Learning The Ropes

A Basic Guide to Safe and Fun S/M Lovemaking

Race Bannon

Foreword by Guy Baldwin

 Daedalus Publishing Company
4470-107 Sunset Boulevard, Suite 375
Los Angeles, CA 90027

Published by Daedalus Publishing Company, 4470-107 Sunset Boulevard, Suite 375, Los Angeles, CA 90027.

Cover design by Don Mooring

ISBN 1-881943-07-0

Library of Congress Catalog Card Number: 92-73484

Printed in the United States of America

Learning
The
Ropes

To all those brave individuals
who have blazed the trail
leading to erotic freedom.

I salute you all.

ACKNOWLEDGEMENTS

No one writes alone. I thank Guy Baldwin for encouraging me to write about S/M and guiding me with loving honesty. Wes Lockwood and Andrew Irish deserve credit for being part of my life as I was learning so much of what this book contains. I want to thank Karen Kircher, Gayle Rubin and Nan Borrows for connecting me to the womens' and heterosexual S/M communities. Tony DeBlase has been inspirational in my desire to educate the masses about S/M. Thanks to Richard Sauer-Wooden for the book's title. My father raised me as an independent thinker and I will always love him for that. To Kevin Lockwood, my closest and dearest friend, for simply being there whenever I needed him. To my partner, Mike Pierce, for his constant support. And to my editor, Richard Labonte, for his expertise.

TABLE OF CONTENTS

FOREWORD

It has always been mystifying to me that human cultural groups are so intolerant of behavioral diversity. Nowhere does this intolerance reveal itself more dramatically than when one group evaluates and then condemns the erotic behaviors of another group simply because they are different.

Honesty about one's erotic differentness risks condemnation. Consequently, the erotically diverse have tended to hide this truth about themselves. Isolation has been the unhappy result for all the erotic minorities: homosexuals, fetishists, sadomasochists, and others. Simply put, hiding in closets is toxic and produces emotional pain.

Truth — accurate information, has proven to be the single most valuable tool for unlocking and opening the closet doors behind which the erotic minorities have sought safety at such a terrible price. As useful information has become available to the erotic minorities, their isolation from each other and from the rest of the world has slowly begun to end. This happy development has been made possible by a dedicated and brave vanguard of social scientists, journalists, publishers, and writers who have been willing to come forward with the truth about the realities of erotic diversity.

In this honest and simply written book, Race Bannon provides an easy-going invitation into the experience of S/M eroticism for those who are interested in exploration there. No one else has attempted to open a doorway into this erotic style in such a gentle way. Take your time as you read what follows, and try to think carefully about what Race is sharing with you, and especially the spirit in which he shares it.

Guy Baldwin, M.S.
Marriage and Family Therapist

PREFACE

About 20 years ago I first became aware of S/M and my attraction to it. Embracing these newfound feelings was difficult. I attepted to reject them repeatedly, but to no avail. Luckily, my erotic interests spanned a broad spectrum and I was able to distract myself with a variety of other sexual interests. But S/M still held its fascination for me.

As one might test the temperature of bathwater, I eased into S/M play slowly and with a great deal of caution. My first few experiences were not good. Not dangerous or unsafe, but not satisfying. These first experiences slowed down my explorations. I retreated to the comfortable sexuality I already knew well. My S/M interests were put on a back burner.

Inevitably, my desire for S/M again emerged and I ventured forth into the world looking for that then elusive magical experience I knew was possible with S/M. One day I found it.

Specifics about that milestone S/M encounter are irrelevant, but its importance in my life is not. I had finally found what I was looking for. I discovered that S/M could be profoundly satisfying. Once the elements of a satisfying S/M experience were known to me, I was able to have them with great regularity.

Perhaps the most important insight gained from those first few positive experiences was the dispelling of myths that I, along with most people, had come to believe about S/M. The realization that S/M could be part of a healthy, loving relationship and that it could be done in a safe and fun way was a breath of fresh air after the staleness of stereotypes and prejudice I had previously accepted as fact.

Finally, my erotic self was set free.

Later, I joined an S/M support organization. The group gathered regularly to discuss various aspects of S/M in a mutually supportive and nonjudgmental way. I soon discovered that many others were having a difficult time accepting and learning about S/M, as I had previously. They believed the myths too. As I began to participate in these discussions, I found myself increasingly helping others learn about safe and fun S/M.

Soon I was asked to lead one of these support groups. Before that evening was through I knew I had something to contribute and the course of my life changed drastically.

Since that time I have devoted a large part of my life to educating others about S/M as I continue to learn more about it myself. I have taught workshops, led support groups, written magazine articles, sat on the board of directors of S/M organizations, and spoken to thousands of people across the country about S/M. This book is a natural next step.

If, after reading this book, you have suggestions or comments, please write to me in care of the publisher. Authors, just like readers, should always keep learning. Perhaps your insights will contribute to a better future edition.

May the teachings in this book help you discover the joys of safe and fun S/M. Play and love well.

Race Bannon

Chapter 1

INTRODUCTION

S/M has long been a much misunderstood style of erotic play. To the uninformed, it appears to be violent, brutal and demeaning. But those who truly understand S/M know that it is a sensual and loving act between the partners involved. Erotic experiences should always contribute to the growth of a person. S/M, if practiced correctly and with love, does just that.

Because S/M is so misunderstood, few people have been willing to put or capable of putting into print information that so many people need. Thankfully, that is beginning to change. In recent years, many new books and magazines aimed at an S/M audience have emerged. This book will hopefully contribute to that growing list and help newcomers more comfortably enter an enjoyable erotic territory.

Although instructional information about S/M could fill volumes, this book has intentionally been kept brief. It is indeed a *basic* guide to S/M. No pretense of completeness is suggested. It offers to newcomers, specifically, a concise overview of basic S/M concepts, techniques and practices. Many seasoned S/M veterans, however, will undoubtedly find it helpful. A lifetime of enjoyable erotic play can be derived from putting into practice what one will read here. However, those who wish to pursue their S/M educations further are encouraged to utilize some of the many resources now available.

Much of the writing about S/M targets specific audiences such as gay men, lesbians, or heterosexuals. This book is generally universal and applies to all sexes and orientations, unless otherwise noted. It is also important to point out that S/M, like all sexualities, is an expression of one's individuality. Therefore, readers are encouraged to take in this information, digest it, and form their own unique style of expression. Creativity and individuality are vital to an enjoyable sexuality. S/M is no different. Read this book. Assimilate it. Then take that knowledge and mold it to fit your own particular erotic style. Remember, no one understands your sexuality better than yourself.

A wise man in the S/M community uses a wonderful metaphor to illustrate people's individual erotic choices. He likened sexuality to a smorgasbord. While there may be a seemingly endless variety of foods on the table, few people like them all. And there's no need to. One can pick and choose those which one likes and leave the others for people with different tastes. The goal is to have an enjoyable meal, not to try everything on the table.

Just as with gastronomic tastes, sexual tastes also vary. Some like spaghetti and some like egg rolls. And some like both. No choice is better than the other. It's all a matter of personal preference.

Each individual reading this book has a different reason for doing so. Many have had S/M fantasies for years and have had no intelligent resource to turn to for a clear explanation of how to turn those fantasies into reality. Others may have some experience with S/M, but find something lacking. Still others may simply want to spice up the lovemaking with their spouse or partner. Whatever the reason, this book can help.

16

The often mysterious nature of S/M is, to many, part of its appeal. There may be those critics who believe that exposing the inner workings of S/M to the general public will demystify the experience and lead to its demise. I totally disagree. Imagination, that wonderful human ability, is a vital ingredient of all good S/M. The imagination can create any reality it wishes. Knowing how to create the S/M experience in a safe and fun way can only increase its enjoyment. Not knowing how, however, can lead to bad S/M experiences. These bad experiences often push newcomers away, thereby depriving them of a form of sexual expression they might have otherwise found fulfilling.

Telling the truth is, ultimately, always the right thing to do. This book tells the truth about S/M; at least the truth as I see it.

Chapter 2

THE SENSUAL
WORLD OF S/M

Welcome to the wonderful world of S/M. If you are new to S/M, you will undoubtedly be pleasantly surprised at what you are going to read. S/M is fun! If it's not, you're doing something wrong. And that is the approach this book takes.

If you're not so new to S/M, this book will most likely validate what you already know. And that's valuable too.

Erotic fantasy is a playground for grownups. When a child plays there is no end to what their imagination can create. A box becomes a playhouse, a wagon becomes a racecar, and a stuffed animal a ferocious dragon. Inside every adult is a child who also loves to play. If you combine that childlike desire to play with the adult sex drive, you have a limitless fantasy life that can keep you and your partner deeply satisfied.

Imagine the possibilities!

And that's what this book is about — possibilities. It's about you and your partner creating endless possibilities in your erotic life. In order to do this you must always remember one thing — there's no such thing as a bad fantasy. That doesn't mean you should actually do everything in your fantasies. It just means that there's nothing wrong with thinking them.

Of course, many of your fantasies can be realized. This

book concentrates on those fantasies involving S/M. Not sure what S/M is? Well, read on.

What is S/M, Anyway?

The term "S/M" (or S&M, both are commonly used) is not an entirely accurate name for the type of sexuality we are exploring here. The abbreviation S/M is derived from the word "sadomasochism," which means the deriving of enjoyment from the infliction and/or receiving of pain. However, the term S/M, as it is now commonly used, has come to encompass a very wide range of erotic activities that do not necessarily involve pain at all. Indeed, it is probably accurate to say that the majority of people into S/M do not enjoy pain, per se.

If pain is not the key element of S/M play, then what is? What makes one erotic encounter S/M and another not? The answer is power. The component that seems to be part of all S/M play is not any particular kind of physical activity, but rather the fact that there is an exchange of power between the partners.

Sometimes this power exchange is very dramatic and other times it is more subtle. The degree of power exchange is not important so long as the experience is enjoyed. If an exchange of power, to whatever extent, takes place, the encounter can be considered S/M in nature.

Let's examine some power exchanges that might be incorporated into one's erotic fantasy life (remember, these are fantasies, not necessarily reality).

- Two partners sign a two week long erotic slavery contract. For a week one partner must be completely devoted to the erotic needs of the other. At the end of the first week, the roles reverse and the pampered one now becomes slave to the other.

- A spouse leaves a note for their partner to be read upon arriving home from work. It orders them to shower, prepare the bed, dim the lights, and be waiting naked in bed for the spouse's arrival.

- A police officer pulls over a traffic violator. In order for the driver to get out of the ticket, he must perform some wonderful sexual act. (Which of course, they enjoy immensely.)

- A lover allows their partner to tie them down on their bed and tickle them mercilessly.

- A doctor makes a patient submit to a very "thorough" examination. (Who knows where those hands might go?)

- A severe figure dressed in black leather commands a large collections of slaves. Luckily, their partner is one of them. (So what if there are really no other slaves. Remember, imagination has no bounds.)

- A strict school teacher administers a severe spanking to a misbehaving student.

- A partner wears a thin chain around their neck that is fastened with a lock, symbolizing their submission and love for their partner. The chain is worn under clothing and is only seen by the two partners in private. The other partner, of course, has the only key.

21

- One partner has abducted the other and is keeping them bound with ropes on their bed. The captive strains to get free.

We could go on and on. If two people care about each other and engage their erotic imaginations, there's no telling what wonderful S/M scenarios they can dream up. That's so much of the fun.

Remember, the fantasies above are just that — fantasies. What might be appealing in an erotic fantasy might be appalling in actuality.

This broader definition of S/M as an exchange of power greatly expands the classically accepted definition and thereby includes a great many people who may not previously have considered themselves into S/M. A common example is that many people are into physical restraint (bondage) as an erotic outlet. Bondage would not be considered a part of S/M as classically defined, but bondage enthusiasts have long been considered an integral part of the S/M community. Actually, even traditional missionary position sex can move into the realm of S/M if the partners have exchanged power with each other.

In the next chapter you will read how some people might exchange power in various kinds of S/M situations.

S/M as Lovemaking

Yes, S/M play is lovemaking. That's a strange concept for many new to the S/M scene. But it's always true. Even if the partners don't know each other very well, their S/M play is a way to express love. As Henry Havelock Ellis, a pioneering writer and researcher of S/M, wrote:

22

"The masochist desires to experience pain, but he generally desires that it should be inflicted with love; the sadist desires to inflict pain, but in some cases, if not in most, he desires that it should be felt as love."

Ellis died in 1939, so his views of S/M were relatively crude. He did not yet see the broader definition of S/M that we embrace today. If he were still alive he would undoubtedly refer to the concept of "power exchange" rather than "pain." Still, the gist of his quote is clear. S/M is motivated by love. S/M is lovemaking.

Safe, Sane and Consensual — The S/M Credo

S/M has had a bad rap for a long time. Some of this is due to those few individuals who partake in improper erotic behavior and call it S/M. But most of the bad rap stems from ignorance. In an effort to eradicate this ignorance, both among the public at large and in their own ranks, the S/M community has adopted a credo by which it lives and plays — safe, sane and consensual. In other words, if it's not safe, if it's not sane, and if it's not consensual, it's not S/M. Any activity that does not meet these criteria is denounced by responsible members of the S/M community. And those people who violate this credo are shunned and avoided by others in the community.

What is safe? Here are some basic S/M safety guidelines:

- Do not exchange dangerous body fluids with your partners. In other words, safe sex or no sex.

- Get to know your partner as well as possible before you play. The intimacy required for enjoyable S/M experiences usually requires a good deal of trust between partners. This doesn't happen right away. Get to know each other.

- Never try to do something that you're not ready for. Certain kinds of S/M encounters require a proficient level of technical skill. Get the necessary knowledge first. Reading this book is a good first step.

- Always be aware of the health and physical safety of everyone concerned. Exchanging health and medical information is a good idea. A CPR and first aid class might be helpful.

- Is your S/M play contributing in any way to a person's negative self-image? It should not. S/M play should build a person up, not break them down.

In short, do whatever is necessary to ensure that the experience will be a safe one. Safety is so important that an entire chapter is devoted to it later in this book.

What is sane? Sane is a relative term. Many people think people into S/M are not sane simply because of this interest. Being sane, as we mean it here, is about using your best judgment. Does it seem "sane" to you personally? Trust your gut feelings and intuition. Sometimes we think only with our genitals, and that can be dangerous. When in doubt, don't.

Sanity also means that those people involved are not under the excess influence of drugs or alcohol. Safety often goes right out the window when someone is high.

It's better to wait until everyone has complete control of their faculties before pursuing any S/M play.

What is consensual? Everyone involved in the S/M situation must consent to all that is transpiring. No exceptions. This also means that everyone has the ability to communicate clearly during the play and that all communications are heeded. Anything that is done against someone's will is an act of rape. And rape is not S/M. Rape is violent, criminal and abhorrent to any responsible person in the S/M community.

As with so many things, there's a lot to consider when pursuing S/M. Knowing the safe, sane and consensual credo allows you to quickly assess situations without remembering long lists of do's and don'ts. Just think to yourself, "is this safe, sane and consensual?" If it is, then go for it. If it's not, make it so or don't do it.

Add Fun to the S/M Credo

When the S/M community adopted the safe, sane and consensual credo, I was overjoyed. It serves its purpose well. But I've always thought it lacked one thing — fun.

S/M is supposed to be fun. If it weren't, why would anyone do it. So I want to add the word "fun" to the credo. So now, ask yourself "is this safe, sane, consensual and fun?" By doing so, you'll ensure yourself not only safe experiences, but fun and fulfilling ones as well.

Why Do People Enjoy S/M?

The only honest answer to this question is "no one knows," although many people have their opinions. Sexuality researchers have been struggling with finding answers to why people enjoy the erotic pleasures they do, but most answers are merely educated theories.

And is it really important to know why you enjoy something? Is it necessary to know why you like chocolate ice cream better than vanilla? Of course not. You simply accept it and enjoy your favorite flavor. So it is with sexuality.

Your sexuality is your own business. As long as what you do is safe, sane, and consensual, it's just fine.

Also remember that a sizable percentage of the population enjoys S/M play. You are not alone.

Misconceptions About S/M

S/M play is fueled by fantasies. The goal of S/M is to turn those fantasies into a safe, sane, consensual and fun reality. Often someone's fantasy may appear as something quite different to an outsider. For example, what if you stumbled onto a movie set without noticing any of the lights, cameras, or crew. If you then saw two actors fighting angrily with fists flying, you would assume you had stumbled onto a real fight. You would have no way of knowing that it was not real. This is what it is like when someone not knowledgeable about S/M hears about or sees an S/M situation. They immediately assume the reality in front of them, not the fantasy it represents. This is the main reason there are so many misconceptions about S/M.

Here are just a few of those misconceptions:

- *S/M is a violent act.* No act done with love and caring can be considered violent. And what perpetrator of violence takes the time to consider the safety and enjoyment of the other person? S/M is not violence. It is another way to make love.

- *S/M is unsafe.* S/M is anything but unsafe. By definition, S/M must be safe or it's not S/M. Responsible S/M players always make sure the experience is a safe one.

- *S/M is demeaning to women.* First of all, the assumption here is that women are always in the submissive role in S/M, and that is just not so. Men and women appear to favor dominant and submissive roles equally. Actually, most enjoy both at one time or another. It may seem that men are always the more dominant when one looks to the S/M pornographic magazines, but that is only because such magazines cater mostly to heterosexual men — they are the ones who buy most such pornography — not because the magazines reflect life as it really is.

  Secondly, the hidden assumption in this misconception is that submission is somehow demeaning. Nothing could be further from the truth. A dominant/submissive relationship is a carefully negotiated, safe, and caring exchange between partners. Is it demeaning when you care so much for someone that you want to make their fantasies come true? Of course not.

  A person cannot be demeaned when they are being loved and cared for. S/M is not demeaning to women (or men).

- *S/M is about pain.* An erotic encounter can have absolutely no pain whatsoever and be considered S/M.

27

S/M is not about pain. It is about a loving and caring power exchange between partners. Forget the word pain and replace it with the word "sensation."

- *S/M cannot be part of a healthy relationship.* Since S/M is just another way to make love, it is at its best when it is done within the context of a loving, caring relationship.

There are many more misconceptions about S/M than those listed above. As people become more educated, attitudes will hopefully change. These new perceptions will make it much easier for those wishing to enjoy S/M play to accept it as a healthy expression of their sexuality.

The S/M Scene

When two or more people have an S/M erotic encounter, it is called a "scene." A more precise definition of what a scene is would be:

A combination of mental, physical and/or environmental components, with an exchange of power as a key element, that mix in such a way as to produce a satisfying erotic experience for all participants.

A scene can be as short as five minutes or as long as a weekend. Some last longer. Regardless of its length, if it meets the above definition, it's a scene.

Scenes don't just begin when you walk into the bedroom. Scenes can happen anywhere and they can begin long before the "action" starts and end long after the action ends. After all, the focus of much S/M play is the mind, not the genitals. Sex may, or may not, be part of a scene. That means that the two people sitting next to you in a restaurant might be in the middle of an S/M scene and you wouldn't know it. Isn't that fun to think about?

A scene is your own erotic theater, where you create your own fantasy world. No two scenes are ever the same. That's one of the great joys in the S/M experience.

Let's see what just a few of the erotic possibilities are by sharing the experiences of some couples in the next chapter.

Chapter 3

S/M IN THE
REAL WORLD

An S/M scene is difficult to describe. The definition in the previous chapter is a bit academic and does not adequately illustrate the limitless variety of S/M play. Perhaps some "real life" examples will help.

Below are descriptions of some S/M scenes between various partners. No two are the same. Although these are a small sampling of the many types of S/M play possible, they do serve to illustrate the kind of safe, sane, consensual and fun S/M that this book supports. By seeing how these partners make love with S/M, the reader will come to a better understanding of S/M and how it can be practiced.

The stories that follow are different from much of the S/M fiction available. Most such fiction is pure fantasy and is not instructive or meant to be imitated. In fact, some fantasies in S/M fiction are downright dangerous and do not adhere to the safe, sane and consensual credo. Science fiction, murder mysteries, and romance novels, among others, intentionally depict stories that are pure fantasy and not a reflection of life. So it is with much of S/M fiction.

Additionally, the stories are not presented as great erotic literature. While the reader may find them titillating, they are meant to be primarily educational.

Since this book caters to all sexes and sexual orientations, the scenes described below take place between various combinations of sexes and orientations. You will find, however, that most of these scenes could be done by any combination of partners with equally satisfactory results. The important thing to notice is the love, care, and erotic imagination these partners display. The sexes and orientations of the partners are, for the most part, irrelevant.

May the sharing of these erotic S/M adventures be the springboard for your own. Set your imaginations free. Read, enjoy and be inspired.

Mark and Janet

Mark and Janet have been married for 17 years. Wishing to keep their erotic life exciting and being a couple who communicate well, they have confided many of their erotic fantasies to each other. It turns out they both have S/M fantasies. They have incorporated these into their lovemaking. Tonight is going to be one of those nights.

Before Janet left for work, she got up early to begin preparations for the night's fun. While Mark slept, she wrote him a note, placed it in an envelope and left it on his briefcase. She then quietly left the house.

When Mark awoke, he followed his usual morning pattern. As he was about to leave for work he went to his briefcase and noticed the note. He opened it. It read,

"My Dearest Mark - I will be home late tonight. This will give you plenty of time to prepare for my arrival. When you arrive home, I want you to shave, shower, and groom yourself to look your best. I then want you to turn down the bed. In the bedroom closet is a small box. Take the rope from that box and place it on the bed. After you have done all this, I want you to wait, naked, on the bed. Do not leave the bed until I arrive home. Do as I ask. P.S. I love you. Janet"

Mark had a smile on his face as he finished the note. He loved his wife very much and looked forward to their lovemaking. Getting through the workday would be easy now. He had a lot to look forward to.

When Mark arrived home he immediately did as the note had asked, then waited anxiously for his wife's return. He didn't have long to wait.

Mark heard the door open and close, then a few footsteps, then nothing. Mark waited what seemed an eternity. Finally, after hearing a few more footsteps, he saw his beautiful wife standing in the doorway. She was wearing her sexiest lingerie and tall high heels. Mark loved her dressed that way, and she knew it.

Janet walked toward the bed. Mark was practically salivating with excitement. Janet leaned over the bed and began slowly and softly stroking her husband's body. Mark's excitement grew, along with another particular part of his body. Then Janet positioned Mark so that he was on his back with his arms and legs spread out to the four corners of the bed.

Janet said, "Don't move. Understand?"

"Yes, I understand," said Mark. "I'll stay still, for you."

Janet now leaned over and began kissing and licking Mark's body head to toe. This continued for a long time and Mark began to writhe with pleasure. Part of him wanted to reach out and touch his wife, but he stayed still, as she had ordered. Janet then began to concentrate her attentions on that part of him that was now very hard and standing straight up. She brought him close to orgasm, then stopped.

"Not yet, my darling. That will happen when I say so," she said.

Janet now began to tie Mark's wrists and ankles to the four corners of the bed. She tied them carefully so that they were secure, but not so tight as to cut off circulation.

"How does that feel?", she asked.

Mark nodded his head that it felt fine. He loved it when his wife tied him up. It always felt as if he were giving himself completely to her at those times. He felt that way now.

With Mark restrained, Janet backed away slightly from the bed and began to undress, very slowly, teasingly. First, she removed her bra.

"Do you like that, my darling?

Mark pulled at the ropes to reach for his wife, but he was going nowhere. His excitement grew.

Next, she unclipped her garters, removed her high heels, and slowly began to roll down her stockings, one at a time. Now, came the panties. She began to pull them down, lingering around the hips for a moment before taking them off. Mark stared lovingly at her now naked body as she walked toward him and climbed onto the bed.

She straddled him and put him inside her. They each let out a moan of delight. In long, prolonged strokes she began to ride him. Each got caught up in the rapture of the moment and strokes became faster and faster, until they each stiffened in mutual orgasms that seemed to go on for an eternity. They collapsed in sweet exhaustion. Janet leaned down and kissed her husband.

"I love you," she said.

"I love you too," was the reply.

They lay there together, still breathing hard, for a few minutes. Then, Janet began to untie the ropes, kissing and rubbing Mark's wrists as she did so.

Once Mark was untied, they wrapped their arms around each other and kissed. Another wonderful scene. They looked forward to many more.

Bob and Jack

Bob and Jack met in a gay leather bar about a year ago and have been seeing each other ever since. From the start it was evident that both wanted a special kind of erotic experience that neither had been able to find before. They see each other once or twice a month and seem to enjoy it that way. No serious discussions of a permanent, committed relationship have emerged, at least not yet.

These men enjoy both the dominant and submissive roles in S/M scenes. Over time, it appeared evident that the type of scenes they most enjoyed were those involving master/slave dynamics.

Both Bob and Jack had fantasies for years about being a master or a slave, but had found no one they could trust to explore this area of their sexuality with. Now they have.

At first they discussed various ways to decide who would be the master and who the slave in a scene. Over time they decided to simply alternate roles each time they see each other. This seems to have worked pretty well thus far. Tonight Bob is to be master.

When they meet, it's always at Bob's place. Bob has a growing collection of S/M equipment and a small, second bedroom he has converted into an S/M playroom. Jack arrives at Bob's this evening at 8 p.m. excited about being Bob's slave for the night. They have not discussed what is to transpire. The trust they have developed allows them that luxury. Each knows he can fully trust the actions of the other. The sense of mystery adds to the excitement. Jack presses the doorbell.

Bob answers. Jack is standing at the door with his head bowed slightly in submission.

"Come in," says Bob.

Jack does so and stands, head still bowed, awaiting Bob's orders.

Bob says, "Go to the playroom, strip, and wait for me. I'll be there shortly."

Jack does as ordered.

When Jack enters the playroom his eyes immediately spot a whip laid out in the center of a small table. Jack has never seen this piece of S/M equipment before. Bob and Jack have had many discussions about exploring whipping scenes. Perhaps Bob took these discussions to heart and purchased a whip for their explorations. Jack hopes so.

Quietly Bob enters the room and moves behind Jack. Bob's hands reach around to the front and begin to play gently with Jack's nipples. Jack lets out a sigh and says, "yes sir, I'm yours." Bob continues to play with Jack's nipples, increasing the pressure slightly over time. Within minutes Jack's nipples are on fire with a splendid sensation somewhere between pleasure and pain, but better than either. Bob soon senses from Jack's responses that he has reached Jack's limit and eases off.

Reaching behind him, Bob produces a blindfold and puts

36

it on Jack. Soft, rhythmic music begins to play as Bob
turns on the stereo system. Jack then feels leather wrist
restraints being put on his wrists. Then Jack's arms are
raised above his head and secured to bolts in the ceiling.
Bob moves close to Jack and begins to talk softly in his
ear.

"Tonight you're going to be whipped. Do you
understand that, boy?"

"Yes, sir."

"And why can I do this to you?"

"Because I belong to you, sir. You can do whatever
you wish with me."

"Are you scared, boy?"

"Yes, a little, sir."

"Good. I like you that way. But you know you can
trust me, don't you, boy?"

"Yes, sir."

"Do you remember our special word?"

"Yes, sir."

"Say it."

"Mercy, sir."

"Correct. I will do as I wish with you unless I hear that
word. If I hear that word, I stop."

"Yes, thank you, sir."

Bob backed away and watched Jack for a moment. How
handsome he looked tonight. How much he would enjoy
this. He reached for the whip on the table. Slowly he
began to run the tails of the whip across Jack's back.
Lightly. In long strokes. Jack's body twitched with
desire. He had fantasized about this for a long time.

Bob had decided to whip Jack's back because he knew
that's what turned Jack on in his fantasies. The first strike
of the whip was light and landed on the fleshy upper

portion of Jack's back. Bob stepped back for an instant to assess Jack's reaction. Jack's body writhed with the pleasure movements Bob had come to know so well. And Jack uttered a contented sigh. Bob knew Jack was ready for more.

Bob began to whip Jack slowly in progressively harder strokes, taking care to watch Jack's reactions all the while. At one point a hard blow landed and Jack's body reacted in a jerky, uncontrolled way. Bob saw this as a sign of a limit being reached and he temporarily lowered the intensity of the blows. Soon, however, Jack was begging his master for more.

"Please, sir, my back is yours. Torture me as you see fit."

Obviously Jack wanted more. Bob was happy to oblige, for it had long been his fantasy to whip someone like this. Before continuing, Bob felt Jack's hand to make sure they were receiving enough circulation. Bob wasn't sure if they felt cool or not, so he asked Jack, "How are your hands."

"Fine, sir," was the answer.

The whipping continued. Jack's body began to move in sharp reaction to each blow. Loud moans began to emerge uncontrollably from Jack. Since Bob had neighbors close by, he put a leather strap in Jack's mouth so he could bite down if he needed to. This would muffle the sounds somewhat.

Stroke after stroke fell upon Jack's back and both men were climbing together to a euphoric crescendo. Soon the scene came to its natural peak. Bob stopped the whipping. Jack was moaning and breathing quickly. Bob put the whip down and went around to the front of Jack. While Bob held Jack in his left arm he undid the quick release snaps that held the wrist cuffs up. Jack fell limply into Bob's arms.

Bob held Jack like that for a long time. All Jack could bring himself to say was, "Thank you, sir."

Carol and Bill

Carol and Bill met a few weeks ago at a friend's party. The friends hosting the party enjoy S/M themselves and many of those attending the party had a similar interest. Carol and Bill were introduced by the hosts and they hit it off right away.

As they began to talk at the party, it became apparent that Bill generally preferred to be dominant in an S/M scene. Which was just fine with Carol. She preferred to be submissive. The chemistry seemed to be there, so they arranged a date for the following week.

Prior to their date, they had many phone conversations in which they discussed, in great detail, their S/M fantasies, past S/M experiences, how they dealt with safe sex, and other important issues. Each also called the couple who introduced them for more information about the other. That couple sang Bill's and Carol's praises and assured both that they were in good company.

Bill and Carol lived near each other so they met at a local restaurant for dinner. Bill knew that Carol liked romance to be an integral part of her S/M experiences. He was waiting at the table when Carol walked into the restaurant. As she approached, he stood, took her coat, pulled out her chair and sat down opposite her. Carol looked down at a beautiful red rose in a bud vase in the center of the table. She looked around and saw that none of the other tables had flowers.

Bill said, "I think the rose is the most beautiful flower

39

in the world. And I think you are the most beautiful woman I've ever met."

Carol sighed silently to herself.

Bill continued. "I want to make love to you this evening in my own special way. To do this, you must give yourself to me completely and you must do this freely and with no fear. I will know when you take the rose from the vase that you give yourself to me. That is the only communication of your submission you need make. I will decide at that point how the rest of the evening shall unfold. Think carefully. Once you take the rose, you are mine for the evening."

Carol was dumbstruck. No man had ever handled her quite so well. He knew all the buttons to push. She thought for a moment about letting dinner progress a while before she took the rose, but that would have been dishonest. She knew her answer now. She reached out and took the rose.

Bill smiled and said, "I will order for you. You need not look at your menu."

He opened his menu and began reading. A moment later he looked up.

"By the way, I meant what I said. You are the most beautiful woman I've ever seen. I'm glad you're mine tonight."

He resumed reading. Carol smiled and quietly waited for her dinner to be ordered. She knew this was going to be a wonderful evening.

Lisa and Carol

Lisa and Carol, life partners for many years, are on vacation. Well, sort of. Lisa had a business convention to go to and Carol came along. During the day Lisa attended the convention while Carol toured the city. But at night, they played together.

While S/M was not a steady interest of theirs, they had come to enjoy it more and more regularly during their lovemaking. It added variety to their sex life and kept the romance alive. They enjoyed the more sensual aspects of S/M and didn't particularly care for very intense role playing. As they put it, they liked their S/M "light and fun." But they did enjoy some element of dominance and submission, and they agreed that they preferred Carol to be in control.

Lisa had called Carol earlier in the day to voice her desire for some S/M play tonight. Lisa pointed out that they had not packed any of the S/M toys they had collected over the years. Carol told Lisa not to worry. After they hung up, Carol called the front desk of the hotel and asked if there were any drugstores or hardware stores around. The hotel manager told her of a grocery store and a drugstore, but he knew of no hardware store in the vicinity.

So Carol went shopping. By afternoon's end she had bought a few items that were sure to prove exciting this evening. But she still wanted one more thing, so she called the hotel manager again and asked if they had any old bedsheets. They did, and the hotel manager offered to have one sent up to her room.

When Lisa arrived back at the hotel she was excited. Carol had a very creative mind. So when she opened the door to the hotel room she had to smile. Carol was standing there, naked. The room was lit with the warm glow of candlelight, and soft classical music emanated from the small radio on the nightstand. Carol walked to Lisa and slowly began to undress her. They were silent, communicating only by looking into each other's eyes. Without a word, simply by quickly assessing Carol's manner, Lisa knew Carol wanted to call the shots tonight.

After Carol had undressed Lisa, she told her to lie on the bed, face up. Lisa did as she was told. After a long day battling with corporate hotshots it was nice to let someone else hold the reins for a while.

Carol produced a bottle of oil she had scented with a few drops of Lisa's favorite perfume. After pouring a bit of the oil into her hand, Carol began to massage Lisa's body. Her hands moved up and down, hovering most of the time around Lisa's breasts and vagina. As Carol had hoped, Lisa began to moan. Lisa's body glistened in the candlelight.

Carol reached under the bed and produced strips of sheeting she had cut from the old bedsheet. Carol knew Lisa didn't like being tied with rope, but instead preferred very soft restraint. The sheeting was a good choice. Carol began to tie Lisa's wrists together. Then the ankles. She then used long lengths of the sheeting to secure the ankles to the foot of the bed and the wrists to the head. With another sheeting strip she blindfolded Lisa. All the while Lisa writhed with anticipation. Carol leaned down and kissed her.

Carol let Lisa lie there, bound and helpless, knowing it would build her anticipation. Then, without a word, Carol got a toothbrush she had purchased and lightly touched it to Lisa's body. Lisa squirmed at the sensation.

Slowly and gently Carol pulled the brush across Lisa's body, making sure to touch as many areas of Lisa's body as she could. From Lisa's forehead to her toes, Carol moved the brush slowly and methodically. At first, both the sensation and Lisa's reaction was mild. But soon the scene intensified as Carol continued. Lisa now pulled against the restraints in response to what she was feeling. Did this tickle? Or was this torture? The sensations were building so fast that Lisa couldn't decide. All she knew was that she liked it.

Carol produced a second toothbrush and began to brush each nipple lightly, both at the same time. Lisa's reaction increased. This sensitive area of her body was on fire with delight. Then Carol slowed the brushes, and then eventually stopped.

Lisa was breathing fast and hard as she recovered from the brushing. She could hear Carol moving around, but couldn't see her. That made the anticipation of what Carol was going to do to her next all the more intense.

Carol grabbed one of the candles from the nightstand. She stood on the bed and held it high over her head, then dripped a single drop of hot wax on the spot between Lisa's breasts. Lisa let out a startled scream. Carol waited a moment, and then delivered another drop, this time to the top portion of Lisa's left breast. Another scream.

The screams were mostly for effect. Lisa actually loved the feeling of hot wax on her body. To her it felt like warm rain. But she also wanted to feel used by Carol, dominated by her, and the quiet screams made that desire real for both of them. Carol continued waxing Lisa's breasts, finishing with two drops on the tips of Lisa's nipples. Lisa yelped and pulled hard against the restraints. Carol found the yelping sound comical, and laughed. Lisa laughed in response.

Carol put the candle down and removed the blindfold. Lisa looked up at Carol and laughed again. They kissed each other as Carol untied Lisa with one hand while the other hand reached between her legs. Soon Lisa was loose and the couple was rolling around in bed, oblivious to anything but their bodies and how good they felt together.

Michael and Richard

Michael and Richard have been life partners for 10 years. Both were interested and experienced in S/M before they met and S/M is an important part of their relationship. Although both have experienced and enjoyed both dominant and submissive scenes, Michael has been the dominant partner, and Richard the submissive, since their first meeting. As a matter of fact, Michael and Richard privately define their relationship as that of master and slave. It turns them both on and works for them erotically.

However, over time they have had to redefine what being master and slave meant. When they first met, their roles were very rigidly defined with Michael controlling every moment of Richard's life. And Richard didn't make a move without first checking with Michael. But as they began to fall in love and looked to a long future together, they discussed the wisdom of trying to maintain such intensity in their lovemaking and decided to modify their relationship.

They still consider themselves master and slave, but they define the roles much more loosely. In fact, their life together is pretty much like any other couple's, except when they play. When they play, they once again assume the rigidly defined roles they have come to enjoy so much. Tonight will be one of their play sessions.

Over time, Michael and Richard have developed a way of indicating to each other that they want to play. If Michael wants to play, he places a short length of chain and a lock on a table by the front door. If Richard takes the lock and chain and locks it around his neck, Michael knows Richard wants to play too. If Richard chooses to initiate the play, he places a small leather paddle on the same table. If Michael picks the paddle up, Richard knows that Michael wants to play. Tonight Michael initiated the play and Richard is now moving about the house with the chain locked around his neck, awaiting his master's command.

Michael was busy in the bedroom getting it ready for their S/M play. He removed some of their S/M gear from a drawer under their bed and laid it out so he could see it all clearly. A black cover was put over the bed and the lights were dimmed. A pair of chains were attached to the two bolts they had installed in the ceiling. Voila! Instant dungeon.

Michael and Richard had never wanted to invest either the time or the money in creating a separate playspace. Their bedroom had served that function well and they saw no reason to go to any more trouble. When Michael had the room looking the way he wanted it, he called to Richard.

"Come here. Now."

Richard rushed to abide by his master's command. He paused at the door to the bedroom and quickly stripped off his clothes. When they were to play he was not allowed in his master's presence with clothes on. Once naked, he walked slowly to his master and knelt at his feet, head down.

"What do you wish, sir?"

"See those boots slave?" Michael was pointing to the boots he wore.

"Yes, sir."

"I want them cleaned."

Richard immediately bent down and began licking Michael's boots. Richard was very turned on by boots and Michael knew it. This was a common way for them to start their scenes.

As Richard continued servicing the boots, Michael began to use the riding crop he had been holding, tapping lightly on Richard's behind. Very light taps. First one. Then a pause. Then another...slowly and methodically. Richard responded with a pleased grunt each time the riding crop landed.

"Work your way upwards, slave," commanded Michael.

Richard began licking his way up Michael's left leg. Since Michael was only wearing boots, a leather jock strap, and a leather biker's cap, Richard had lots of skin to taste on his way to Michael's crotch. Michael continued to use the riding crop on Richard — each stroke slightly harder than the last.

Soon Richard reached Michael's crotch and he began to lick the front of the leather jock with a voracious appetite. Michael let him have his treat for a moment, then pulled Richard's head away.

"You'll get what's inside that jock later. If you do as you're told."

"Yes, sir. Thank you, sir," said Richard.

Michael said, "stand up, hands at your side." Richard did so without hesitation. Michael placed him near the bed but facing away from it.

Michael had decided to do a bondage scene with Richard tonight. In particular, a type of bondage called mummification. This would involve the wrapping of Richard's body until it was encased entirely, just like an Egyptian mummy. First, he placed a small towel between

Richard's ankles. This would keep them from rubbing together. Then he took a roll of plastic food wrap and began slowly wrapping Richard's head, being careful to leave both the nose and the mouth uncovered in order not to restrict Richard's breathing.

Once Richard's head was wrapped, Michael turned his efforts to the upper part of his lover's body.

"Take a deep breath," ordered Michael. Richard did. Michael then began wrapping the chest area of Richard's body. After a few wraps around, Michael told Richard to exhale. By wrapping the chest when it was fully expanded, Michael insured that Richard would have plenty of room to breath comfortably while in the bondage. While wrapping the chest, Michael also made sure to leave the nipples uncovered. They would be fun to play with later.

The wrapping continued down Richard's body. Now Richard's arm were held tightly to his side. As Michael was wrapping the middle portion of Richard's body, he left Richard's crotch exposed. That would also be fun to play with later.

As Michael began to wrap Richard's legs together, he paid special attention to Richard's balance. Once Richard's legs were bound together he could easily fall. That's why Michael kept Richard close to the bed. If Richard became unbalanced, Michael would either steady him quickly or push him lightly toward the bed so he could comfortably fall on something soft.

Now Richard was completely encased. And loving it.

Michael said, "how are you doing, slave."

Michael's voice was slightly muffled due to the wrapping, but he could be heard well enough. "Fine, sir."

"I want you to keep your body very stiff, now," said Michael.

Richard did so. Michael then leaned him backwards slowly until Richard was lying on the bed. This was fairly easy for Michael to do because he was so much bigger than Richard. It might be a more difficult task with a much larger slave. Michael positioned Richard lengthwise on the bed and placed a small pillow under Richard's head.

"I'm going to leave for a while, slave. This will keep you right where I want you until I need you. Understand?"

"Yes, sir."

But Michael didn't leave. That would never be a wise thing to do with someone in such restrictive bondage. So Michael pretended to leave, but remained just outside the bedroom door in clear eye sight of Richard lying in bondage. He let Richard lie there for about 20 minutes before he walked quietly back into the room.

He gently pinched Richard's nipples with his hands. Richard's body convulsed. He groaned and began emitting pleasure sounds that made Michael want to do this all the more.

After playing with Richard's nipples for a while with his hands, he gently placed a clothespin on each of them. This would keep Richard's nipples busy while he worked on his crotch.

Michael now grabbed lubricant and squeezed some into his right hand. He began to slowly stroke Richard's already hard cock. More pleasure sounds from Richard.

Michael worked Richard's cock until he was close to ejaculating, then slowed the pace, then built it up again. Each time Richard writhed in sensual agony as his master brought him so close, yet not all the way.

"You want me to go all the way, slave?"

"Yes, sir. Please, sir," begged Richard.

"No" was all Michael said. And he continued his

torment. Again and again he brought Richard close, then slowed the pace. This continued for a long time. But the night was young and Michael had much more in store for Richard.

Mary and Patricia

Mary and Patricia have been dating for over a year. Although they did not initially identify their erotic tastes as S/M, they later learned that they, indeed, were. Their scenes centered around sensual visual images they created together. These visual images were often representative of a subtle power dynamic in their play, thus making that play S/M in nature.

When Mary and Patricia played, they took great care to dress properly. Their undergarments, stockings, shoes, along with the rest of their clothing, were carefully chosen to elicit a particular erotic response from their partner. Their hair and makeup were also carefully done to elicit a similar response.

Tonight Mary had chosen to dress in a powerful, businesswoman fashion, a look she enjoyed. Her grey suit, scarf tie, hair and makeup, along with her poised demeanor, all spoke of a powerful woman in control. Patricia chose to dress in a sultry, sexy manner. She chose very feminine, lacy undergarments and a revealing low cut mini dress. Her hair was loose and free and her makeup just this side of harlot. She wore very high heels that accentuated her long legs.

Neither woman discussed ahead of time how they would dress for the evening. That was part of the fun for them. The two personalities would converge and the resulting sexual chemistry would be spontaneous.

Mary arrived at Patricia's house to pick her up. They had decided that how they dressed should be appropriate for public consumption since they wanted to go out to dinner first. Mary rang the bell and Patricia answered. Each eyed the other for a moment and smiles crossed both their faces. Instant turn on.

"Shall we go?," asked Mary. "The sooner we have dinner the sooner we can come home."

"Yes, I was thinking the same thing," said Patricia.

Phillip and Susan

One day Phillip's girlfriend of six months, Susan, confided to him that she had fantasies about having sex with her male doctor. Her fantasies revolved around her doctor forcing her to do his sexual bidding. She was embarrassed when she told Phillip, but Phillip found it exciting. Phillip and Susan had a very open and free erotic relationship and Phillip was always looking for new ways to spice up their lovemaking. This gave him an idea.

The next day Phillip went to the local thrift shops and found a doctor's smock. He then called a friend who was a nurse and asked if he could borrow some of her medical equipment for an evening. He explained why he wanted it and she was more than happy to make the loan. She even offered to help if she could. When his girlfriend came over that night, Phillip was ready.

Susan rang Phillip's doorbell. The door opened, but instead of seeing Phillip she saw Phillip's female friend, dressed as a nurse, who greeted her.

"Good evening. Please have a seat and the doctor will see you shortly," the nurse said signalling to the living room couch. Without another word, she walked out the front door, closing it behind her.

Phillip was hidden from view, watching this transpire. He let Susan sit for a moment, then entered the living room wearing the smock accessorized with a stethoscope around his neck.

"Good evening, Miss Jackson."

"Phillip, what's going on..."

With some force, "I said, good evening, Miss Jackson. Won't you come into my office." Phillip motioned to the bedroom.

Susan was dumbstruck, but quickly caught on to what Phillip was doing.

"Yes, doctor," she said, with a smile on her face, walking into the bedroom.

"You're scheduled for a complete physical, Miss Jackson, so please remove all your clothing," said Phillip emphasizing the word complete in his tone as he scanned a clipboard with something that looked like a medical chart on it.

"Yes, doctor," said Susan.

Susan undressed and stood there, waiting for the doctor to look up from his reading. Soon he did.

"Please get on the table, Miss Jackson," said Phillip, pointing to the bed. Susan did as he ordered. Phillip then positioned Susan near the edge of the bed with her legs spread slightly and her knees bent.

"Relax, Miss Jackson. This won't hurt at all." Phillip then produced a latex examination glove which he put on his right hand. He dabbed a small amount of lubricant jelly from a tube onto the glove and slowly and carefully inserted his finger into Susan's vagina.

Susan was reeling with excitement. For this brief moment, Phillip was no longer her boyfriend. He was her doctor, the man she had fantasized about for so long. And he was touching her in the way she had always hoped he would in her fantasies.

Phillip began to massage her clitoris gently with his finger. Susan squirmed with ecstasy.

"Please, doctor, stop," said Susan, obviously feigning resistance.

"Just relax, Miss Jackson. After all, I am the doctor."

With that gentle command, Susan settled back and enjoyed the feelings emerging from her loins.

Once again, remember that these are only a small sampling of the potential scenes S/M offers to those wishing to expand their erotic play. There are as many possibilities as your fantasies and imagination can create.

Chapter 4

S/M AS EROTIC THEATER

One way to describe S/M is as "erotic theater" — an intimate, theatrical play created by you and your partner. All the theatrical elements are included. We'll use this theatrical metaphor to explain how an S/M scene happens.

The Script

Without a script, there is no play. So it is with S/M. Some basic structure for a scene must be decided upon prior to the scene beginning. Sometimes this structure is very precise and other times it is more loose, allowing for more improvisation and spontaneity. Either approach can work well, depending on the partners and the type of scene.

When two people come together to discuss the structure of a scene, it is called "negotiating" a scene. Some form of negotiation must always occur before a safe, sane and consensual scene can take place. The negotiation may take only a few minutes or it may take much longer. But negotiation must happen. Here are some questions partners might ask each other when they are negotiating a scene.

• What are some of your S/M fantasies?

Don't try to be a mind reader. Ask about your partner's S/M fantasies. And tell them yours.

53

- What are your safe sex guidelines?

  Although safe sex information has been widely disseminated, people vary in what they consider safe and in the type of safety precautions they wish to take. This is important information. Never compromise your safe sex standards.

- What types of S/M play especially turn you on?

  By asking this question you know immediately those areas of interest you have in common.

- What types of S/M play especially turn you off?

  There's nothing worse than beginning to play with someone only to find out that what you're doing completely turns them off, or what they're doing completely turns you off.

- What kind of experience do you have with S/M play?

  The level of experience you and your partner have is important to know. For example, an experienced S/M player might approach someone new to S/M differently than they would someone with a great deal of experience.

- Where would you like to play? My place? Your place?

  Basic information, but important.

- Would you like to notify someone where you are?

If you are playing with someone for the first time, it's not a bad idea to notify a friend of your whereabouts. A sensitive partner will understand this.

• Are you more dominant or submissive? Do you like to switch?

Knowing which direction the power is to be exchanged is vital, basic information for successful negotiations.

• Do you have any health or physical considerations I should know about?

If a person is asthmatic, wears contacts, has a heart condition, has a cold, or has problems with their bone joints, this is important to know to insure that the play in the scene does not in any way threaten their health or safety.

• How "out" are you about your S/M interests?

Everyone has the right to express their erotic interests to others as much or as little as they wish.

• How long can you play?

People do have lives outside of their erotic playtime and consideration must be given to this. How you approach a scene might differ greatly if someone must be at work in three hours than if they have all weekend to play.

These are just some of the questions that might come up during a negotiation. Many more are possible. You decide on what is important for you to know. No matter which side of the power exchange you're on, you have a right to know everything necessary to feel comfortable during the scene.

You need not approach the negotiation as a checklist of questions to ask. A time of good, open, and honest communication is what's important here. Just make sure you cover the issues that are important to you. How you do that is up to you.

Safe Words and Signals

Some of the other issues you probably need to discuss with a potential S/M partner are safe words and signals. Partners often establish a way of easily communicating with each other during a scene. For example, it might be decided that the submissive partner is to never use the dominant partner's first name. However, if the submissive partner calls the dominant partner by their first name (let's say Jack), that indicates that the scene is going too fast and the submissive partner wishes to slow down the action. In this case, "Jack" is the safe word.

Any word can be a safe word. You could use "slow," "switch," and "stop." Slow would mean slow down the action. Switch would mean everything's OK, but switch to something else. Stop would mean just that, stop everything and let's talk. Use your imagination. Come up with your own safe words.

The value of safe words is that they allow the status of the scene to be communicated quickly and easily, without necessarily interrupting the flow of the scene itself. Stopping a scene and engaging in long discussions disrupts the flow and mood of the scene. Safe words can help avoid this.

Are safe words absolutely necessary? No. Some partners don't use them. However, such partners must make sure to have other ways of communicating during a scene.

Signals are sometimes established, especially if a partner is going to be in a position where they will find it difficult to speak. Such a signal might be the snapping of fingers, which will easily get the other partner's attention, even if their back is turned.

These safe words and signals are very important, especially the first few times you play with someone. Remember, an S/M scene must be entirely consensual. Safe words and signals help maintain that consensuality.

Casting the Roles

Within the script (the negotiation) are the roles each of you will play in the S/M scene. Role decisions are an essential part of the initial negotiation process. Three distinct types of role decisions are usually made. They are *power direction*, *level of control*, and the *S/M persona*.

Power Direction —

In most instances, this is a fairly clear-cut decision. Which direction will the power exchange flow? In other words, which partner is to be more dominant (sometimes called the "top") and which partner is to be more submissive (sometimes called the "bottom"). Often this decision takes care of itself immediately because the partners have definite preferences as to which they prefer. If both partners can go either way, usually a direction is

57

chosen for the specific scene. Of course, in some scenes the power might flow back and forth, if that's what turns on the players.

Level of Control —

Once a decision is made as to who will be the dominant player in the scene, the level of control each person has must be decided upon. Each partner must decide how much control they want and how much control they are willing to surrender. This might appear to be an easy decision. You might believe that the dominant partner will, of course, have total control and the submissive partner will surrender all control completely. This is rarely the case, however, even if the fantasy which the scene is based upon contains this absolute shifting of power and control.

An illustration might help here. Let's say two people have decided they are going to play. The more submissive partner is very experienced in S/M, while the dominant partner is very new to S/M. During negotiations they decide that since the submissive partner has much more experience, that partner will guide the scene and assure that it is done in a fun and safe way. That means that the submissive partner must have a high level of control, even if the "fantasy" of the scene is that the dominant partner has the greater amount of control.

S/M Persona —

The persona that each partner adopts during S/M play is a matter of individual preference. Just a few of the personas people enjoy are master/mistress and slave, coach and athlete, teacher and student, doctor and patient, daddy/mother and son/daughter (in all combinations), torturer and captive, officer and enlisted person, and jailer and inmate.

Actually, most people do not adopt specific personas during S/M play. Rather, they assume qualities of some of these personas. For example, while partners might not actually decide upon the personas of master and slave, they might play out the scene with a lot of the dynamics those personas elicit without specifically identifying their personas as master and slave.

It appears that, by far, the most popular of the classic S/M personas is that of master/mistress and slave. But you should play with whatever personas turn you on, not the ones that are the most popular. Remember, there's no one right way to do S/M, as long as it's safe, sane, consensual, and fun.

The Set

When you play, the environment you play in can affect the scene greatly. Some people's fantasies are directly related to the setting that the fantasy takes place in. For example, if someone has a fantasy of being tied to a tree outdoors, it makes sense to try to do that with a real tree outside, if you can. Of course, finding such private places can be tricky.

Be creative. Your bedroom can be made to look like almost anything — a dungeon, a gym, a doctor's office, whatever. Let your imagination go wild. Just one or two minor changes to a room can transform its appearance. For example, dim the lights, throw a black sheet over your bed and attach a couple of shackles to the bedpost, and you can instantly create a "dungeon".

Remember, a good set need only give an indication of the environment. That most important S/M element, your mind, will fill in the gaps and create the reality you wish.

Props

Many people engage in S/M play without using any props (erotic toys) at all. But most people in S/M, at one time or another, enjoy using some S/M toys (often called "gear" or "equipment"). S/M toys are anything you and your partner use in an S/M scene to enhance the play.

Some common S/M toys are rope, restraints, paddles, whips, nipple clamps, blindfolds, and handcuffs. These are just a few of the many toys available to make your S/M play more exciting. And S/M toys need not be expensive. Later, in the S/M Gear chapter, I'll discuss S/M toys in more detail.

Costuming

Everyone wants to look sexy. And everyone wants their erotic partner to look sexy. In S/M play, your appearance can affect how enjoyable a scene might be.

Many people find certain "looks" erotic. Leather wear, uniforms, gym gear, latex, spandex, and undergarments are just some of the looks that people find appealing. There is no one right way to dress for S/M play. The only right way is the way that appeals to you and your partner.

Some in S/M find the more stereotypical S/M looks a turn off because they take away from the reality of the scene. For these people, playing in their regular clothing, or just naked, might be more appealing. What you wear, or don't wear, is irrelevant, as long as it turns you and your partner on.

The Performance

The S/M scene itself is the performance of your erotic theater piece. You and your partner will put together all the various elements to create your own, unique, and fun S/M scene.

And don't forget, all the world's a stage.

Another Metaphor — S/M As Music

I often describe an S/M scene using another metaphor — music. I am continually fascinated and delighted when I hear the endless varieties of music — all beautiful and yet so different. Think of all the music you have heard and realize that no one will ever create all the music there is to create. Musical creation is limitless. Yet, all music is basically constructed of the same few notes. The difference is the way the notes are arranged, the style of play, the personality, talent and experience of the musician, the environment the music is heard in, and the type of instrument.

It is just so with S/M. Think of the notes as the various kinds of S/M play available (bondage, spanking, roles, etc.), the instruments as S/M toys (including your hands, voice, etc.), the environment as your bedroom, playroom (or wherever), the style of play as how you put the elements together, and, of course, the uniqueness of you.

A good S/M scene is truly like a great piece of music. May you become a great musician.

Chapter 5

DISCOVERING HOW S/M
FITS INTO YOUR LIFE

Where do you fit into the S/M scene? That is up to you. There is room for every interest and degree of participation. The important thing to remember is to reject the misconceptions and stereotypes. Express yourself as an individual. Make S/M work for you. As long as it's safe, sane, consensual, and fun, it's OK.

Begin your exploration of your S/M interests and desires now. The sections below will help.

Masturbation Fantasies

One of the surest ways to discover what kinds of S/M activities turn you on is to explore the contents of your masturbation fantasies. What goes through your mind when you masturbate (assuming you do, of course)? Stand back from these fantasies and examine them closely.

Remember, everything is acceptable in your fantasies. Don't censor them in any way. Just because you fantasize about something does not mean you actually want to do it. It does mean, however, that there is something about that fantasy you find exciting. The key to using masturbation fantasies here is to determine the "essence" of such fantasies which can be safely explored in reality.

The Essence of a Fantasy

One of the reasons people often don't try to make their fantasies a reality is that they see their fantasies too literally. They have a wonderful fantasy, realize they might not be able to duplicate it exactly in reality, and write it off as unattainable. Erotic frustration will most likely result if one continually rejects such fantasies this way.

Instead of rejecting the fantasy, analyze it. What is the essence of the fantasy? The essence of a fantasy is its most significant component. For example, perhaps while masturbating you often fantasize about being kidnapped and forced to submit to sexual acts by your captor. Now, no one would really want this to happen. It's just an erotic fantasy. But that doesn't mean you can't use this fantasy to enhance your erotic life.

If, when you have this fantasy, you always imagine your captor wearing a leather jacket and sunglasses, perhaps the essence of this fantasy for you is the way your captor looks. It is a simple matter for you and your partner to extract this essential element from your fantasy and place it into reality. Your partner can easily wear a leather jacket and sunglasses during a scene, thereby reconstructing the key element of your fantasy during your lovemaking. This may evoke similar sensations and feelings that you have during your fantasy.

Or, perhaps the bondage your captor restrains you with in your fantasy is what you determine really turns you on. By introducing a similar bondage situation in a real life scene, you can also evoke those same feelings.

When searching for the essence of your fantasies, concentrate on how the fantasy makes you feel emotionally, not on the physical action that is taking place. Find the source of your feelings during a fantasy and you'll probably find the essence.

Fantasy Visualization Exercise

The purpose of this exercise is to help you discover what kind of S/M scene you might enjoy under ideal circumstances. This exercise guides you through a visualization of your perfect S/M scene as it might really take place.

In your masturbation fantasy you might enjoy a wide range of fantasies that turn you on, but cannot necessarily be accomplished (or would be too dangerous) in real life. With this exercise, the aim is to visualize an ideal S/M scene as you might like it to really happen. Nothing in your visualization should be unsafe or nonconsensual.

Here's the exercise:

Sit or lie in a comfortable position. Loosen any tight clothing. Close your eyes and begin taking deep, slow breaths. Allow your body to relax completely. Focus first on your feet. Notice the small amount of tension still in them as you inhale slowly. Then feel the last bit of tension release as you exhale slowly. Next, do this with the ankles. Then, the calves. Work your way up the body to the top of your head so you are calm, peaceful and very relaxed.

Now, create in your mind a picture of yourself standing at one end of a long hallway. At the other end of the hallway is a door. Behind that door lies your perfect S/M fantasy. Everything in this fantasy will be just the way you'd like it to be. The person(s) you're interacting with will look and be dressed exactly as you want them to be.

The setting will be exactly where you would most enjoy playing. The power exchange dynamics and roles will be perfect. The style of play and type of play will be just what you would enjoy most. Don't try to think about what this might look like yet. Just believe that on the other side of that door, it exists.

Begin walking down the hall. You are slowly approaching the door, remembering all the while that on the other side is your perfect S/M scene. Closer. Closer. Now, your hand is on the knob of the door and you are about to enter. You are about to enter your perfect S/M scene. Open the door and step inside.

You are now in the midst of your ideal S/M scene. Look around. What do you see? What kind of environment are you in? Are you inside or outside? Who is there with you, if anyone? How do you feel? Are you feeling submissive or dominant? If someone else is there, how do you feel toward them? What kind of a person are they? How are they treating you?

Let the scene proceed. Keep remembering that this scene can be any way you want it to be as long as it's safe, sane, consensual and fun. Don't feel obligated to stay in this visualization for too long. In your mind, speed up time if you like. You can experience a two-hour scene in a matter of minutes if you wish. When the scene comes to an end, take a moment to closely examine your feelings and observations. Then, slowly walk back through your magic door. Close the door behind you and begin walking back down the hallway.

When you reach the point in the hallway you originally started from, you will be wide awake, happy and filled with satisfaction from your great scene.

It's important to realize that each time you do this

exercise your fantasy may be different, and it may not. It's your fantasy and it can be whatever you want it to be.

After you finish your visualization, extract some of the elements that seem particularly appealing. Make a list on paper if that's comfortable for you. Itemize all the elements of the scene you found exciting.

Once you've done that you're ready for the really important part. Go over the elements of the scene and figure out how you can make them come true in real life. Even though you were told to visualize a scene that is entirely safe and consensual, some other fantasy elements might have crept in. You may have to do some adapting, but that's part of the fun. For example, while you might have been getting whipped a little harder in your visualization than is appealing to you in reality, you might be able to find someone who could whip you with a very soft whip that would not cause you any pain. The sensation of them whipping you hard may be enough to bring up the same emotions you were having in the visualization. This kind of adaptation happens all the time in S/M.

Writing Exercise

Take a sheet of paper and make three columns. In the first column, list all those S/M and erotic activities that you know you do enjoy. Write down everything that comes to mind. Don't censor anything. In the second column, list all those S/M and erotic activities you definitely know you do not enjoy. In the third column, list all those S/M and erotic activities that you're not sure about. Referring to the Glossary of this book may help you with your lists.

Now, look at your lists. This will tell you a great deal

about your S/M interests and what kinds of S/M scenes you will want to pursue.

It is also interesting to do this exercise once a year or so. You'll probably notice that certain items have moved to different columns. Activities you thought you didn't like might now be in the column of things you like. Activities you were sure you would like have moved to the column of things you're not sure of. Also, new items have appeared in your columns that were not in any of the three columns previously.

This exercise can be of great help with two partners, as well. Each partner completes their lists and then gives their list to the other. Now each partner has an incredible amount of information as to what turns on (and turns off) their partner. Remember, your erotic partner is not a mind reader. How can you ever expect your erotic fantasies to be fulfilled if your partner doesn't know what they are.

Another column you might want to add to your list is your safe sex guidelines. People have different guidelines for what they consider safe sexual activity. You should have a clear understanding of what yours are as well as your partner's before you play. Perhaps reading the Safety chapter in this book will help to define your safety guidelines more clearly.

Reading

Reading S/M-oriented books and magazines will give you a broad exposure to various kinds of S/M play. This reading may fuel your imagination and allow you to expand your erotic repertoire.

Some S/M publications are geared toward pure fantasy. This kind of S/M fiction can be exciting, but it can also help you decide what turns you on (or off). Other S/M publications are more informational and educational in nature. These are equally important because you need to know how to turn those fantasies of yours into safe realities.

There is a small list of recommended books at the end of this book. Reading these would be a great addition to your continuing S/M education.

Releasing Expectations

One of the main causes of unsatisfactory erotic experiences, in my opinion, is unrealistic expectations. So often we build a fantasy in our mind in great detail and then go out into the world in hopes of making that fantasy a reality. Depending on the complexity and specificity of the fantasy, it may be easy or difficult to bring to fruition. Using visualizations and other types of fantasy experiences may help to illuminate your erotic interests, but don't always pursue them so literally. Use your common sense.

For example, if you're looking for a scene with a 6'6" blond partner, built like a bodybuilder, who speaks with a German accent, who has a fully equipped S/M playroom, who has years of S/M experience, and who knows exactly how to play with you even though you've never spoken to each other, that's pretty unrealistic. I'm not saying it can't happen. It could. But it's not likely.

Loosen up your expectations. Give people a chance. Now I'm not saying you should compromise your standards or try something you know you won't enjoy. Just try to broaden your possibilities. I think you'll be happier for it.

The S/M Community

The networking of people interested in S/M has grown to the point where it can now be said that a true S/M community exists. This S/M community has developed its own culture rich with unique language, dress, artwork, social rituals, etc. Finding your place in the S/M scene is a lot easier if you have help from other S/M community members. Below are some of the more noteworthy developments in the growing S/M movement.

- Men and women in the S/M scene, whether they be heterosexual, bisexual, gay or lesbian, are uniting as one community. The common interest in S/M appears to be more important than the specific sexual orientation. Issues of mutual interest are being addressed as one body rather than by many different factions.

- S/M oriented events are taking place throughout the country with increasing frequency. Workshops, seminars, conventions, dances, contests, rap groups, and play parties are becoming an integral part of the S/M culture. In addition, panels on or discussions of S/M are more than ever a part of events not specifically S/M in nature — literary conferences, health conferences, political gatherings.

- S/M support organizations are sprouting up all over the country. And not just in the major urban areas either. Joining one of these support organizations is a great way to meet like minded people and learn more about yourself and S/M.

- S/M people are communicating with and educating each other more than ever. Whether it is face to face or through magazines, newsletters or books, members of the S/M community no longer feel as though they exist in isolation. They know many others feel as they do and they make sure they keep in touch with those people.

Take advantage of the opportunities available to you in the S/M community. Become a part of it. Get to know others who have similar interests. By talking with and socializing with others, you'll learn more about how you want to fit into the S/M scene.

Evolving in S/M

It is important to realize that your sexuality is an ever evolving thing. Since sexuality is an expression of your individuality and since you, as a person, change, it makes sense that your sexuality will evolve with those changes.

Never restrict the possibilities of your sexuality. Give yourself free reign over the vast and wonderful choices you have in your S/M play. That doesn't mean you have to try everything. Just keep your mind open. As one great saying goes: "A mind is like a parachute. It doesn't work unless it's open."

Finding Resources

When I first began writing this book I had hoped to include an appendix section with a thorough listing of S/M community resources. Such resources would help the newcomer connect more easily with the rest of the S/M community. I wanted to list such things as clubs, organizations, magazines, newsletters, S/M equipment vendors, and national S/M community events, to name just a few.

As I began to compile this list, I realized that such listings change rather quickly. Just as I thought I had completed the list, a new club would be formed or a business would cease operation. I soon realized that any such list would go out of date rather quickly.

Because I am a writer, I made the commitment to provide a recommended reading list in this book. However, to accommodate the need of providing readers with other up to date S/M community resources, I created The S/M Resources Guide. This guide is fully explained in a separate section at the end of this book.

I mention this here because some of the resources listed in the guide might help you discover how S/M fits into your life.

Chapter 6

S/M TECHNIQUE

One of the best things about S/M is its allowance for individual erotic expression. As long as something is safe, sane, and consensual, and done between consenting adults, anything is fair game. The only limitation is one's imagination.

However, within this freedom of expression there are right and wrong ways to do certain things. And in cases where there are many right ways to do something, certain ways may produce more satisfying results than others. What we're talking about here is "S/M technique."

Good S/M technique makes for better scenes.

What is Technique?

When we talk about S/M technique, we're talking about the proper way to do various types of S/M play. Now, no one should be so pompous as to think that they know the one and only right way to do S/M. But there are many technique guidelines that a large part of the S/M community agrees upon.

Some technique guidelines are important because they insure the safety of those playing. These guidelines should be strictly adhered to. There is little room for variation with safety.

Other technique guidelines are generally followed because they produce a more satisfying result for most people, not necessarily for safety's sake. This type of technique can be adapted to fit the needs and desires of the partners in the scene.

In other words, where technique is concerned and safety is an issue, there is no compromise. When the style and approach are an issue, there is much room for negotiation and individual creativity. Once again, remember the S/M credo. If your technique is safe, sane and consensual and everyone is having a good time, all is OK. Let the S/M credo be your guiding light whenever you have questions about your technique. But let's get more specific.

Two Kinds of Technique

There are two broad categories of S/M technique -- physical and mental. Physical technique covers such areas as how to tie someone up properly, how to spank someone for the most satisfying effect, how to handle a whip, and how to properly play with someone's nipples. These are physical activities and proper physical technique is fairly easy to describe. Mental S/M technique is a bit more difficult to pin down, but we'll discuss it briefly in the next chapter.

The S/M Sensation Cycle

Much of S/M technique hinges upon something I call the "S/M sensation cycle." Usually the enjoyment of physical sensations in an S/M scene depends upon understanding this cycle. Being aware of this sensation cycle will enhance all your S/M play.

Here's how the S/M sensation cycle works. This will sound a bit cold and academic, but understanding it will really help.

When a physical S/M scene is taking place, certain events occur in the following cyclical pattern:

- The bottom indicates they are ready to receive the sensation.

- The top administers the sensation.

- The first awareness of the sensation is perceived by the bottom and the type and intensity of the sensation is registered.

- The result of the sensation resonates through the bottom's body and mind.

- A period of recovery takes place. During this period the bottom assimilates the sensation fully. The higher the level of intensity, the longer this recovery period needs to be.

- Once recovery is complete, the bottom signals the top that they are ready for another sensation and, if the top so chooses, another sensation is doled out. During the bottom's signaling, they also indicate verbally, through sounds, or through body language, the pace and intensity at which the next sensation will satisfy them most.

- Having evaluated the bottom's reactions, the top administers another sensation. The cycle then repeats itself until the physical portion of the scene is complete.

An example might illustrate this cycle less dryly. During a scene, a submissive partner says to the other "I would even take a hard spanking to prove my devotion." This is read by the top as a clear signal that the bottom would like a spanking. So, during the course of the scene, the top bends the bottom over their knee and begins to administer a spanking. The top begins with a single light slap. The bottom's body, and mind, immediately register this as a fairly light hand strike and the sensation resonates through the bottom's body. Since the strike was light, the bottom assimilates this blow quickly, then tilts their hips sensually toward the top. The top reads this as a signal that the bottom is ready for the next blow. The top spanks the bottom again. And so on and so on, until both partners are satisfied with the spanking portion of their scene.

Virtually all physical S/M play abides by this sensation cycle, at least to some extent. Sometimes all the above steps happen within seconds. Other times it takes much longer.

What should be clear in the above description is that S/M partners are just that — partners. Each partner gives input that affects how the other partner will play. This back and forth communication, be it verbal or not, is vitally necessary for good S/M. The often idealized fantasy of one person having complete control over the other with virtually no input coming from the submissive partner is great fantasy material, but doesn't usually make for very good scenes.

Types of Physical S/M Play

There are many different kinds of physical S/M play, but most of them fall into a few general categories. These are discussed in detail below.

While reading this section, please remember the following points —

• The categories below are by no means all inclusive. This book is a basic guide and does not purport to talk about all of the many kinds of S/M play possible. I'm not sure any one volume could do that. The types of play listed below are those that are most common among members of the S/M community and, therefore, most appropriately discussed in a basic guide such as this. Look to the glossary for a brief overview of some other types of S/M play.

• Just because you are presented with all these types of play does not mean you have to want to do them. Your sexuality is unlike anyone else's and you get to play with it in any way you wish. Never forget that.

• If your primary interest in S/M is from a submissive/ bottom perspective, you might think you don't need to know about S/M technique. Wrong. A good bottom should know as much about good S/M technique as they can. How else can you assess the technical skills of a top if you don't know how to do it correctly yourself?

Bondage

Bondage, as meant here, is the restraining of the body in some way to produce an enjoyable, erotic effect. Many people who enjoy S/M use bondage to enhance their scenes. And some people enjoy bondage as a scene all by itself.

77

Newcomers to the S/M scene often try bondage first. Providing you're with someone you know and trust, it is relatively nonthreatening because it is perceived as not involving any pain. Of course, you now know that pain is not necessarily the point of S/M at all, but to the newcomer that is not always so clear.

Caution should be exercised where bondage is concerned if you are playing with someone you have met fairly recently. A secure bondage makes the restrained person truly helpless from a physical standpoint. Certainly that is part of its appeal, but it is also the reason for its danger. Never let anyone restrain you unless you are absolutely certain they will release you if you wish it.

For many, bondage serves a utilitarian purpose. It keeps the bottom in place while the top plays with them. With some more experienced players, the bondage might keep the bottom from hurting themselves, or the top. When someone is under the influence of a high dose of stimulation, they may thrash wildly and might hurt themselves or their play partner in the process. Bondage can reduce or eliminate this danger.

For others, bondage can serve as a visual and artistic expression. These players care a great deal about how the bondage looks to the eye. Visual beauty of the bondage (and the person in the bondage) is important to them.

Both ways of using bondage can be fun. Neither way is more correct. And the bondage can be both beautiful to look at and serve the purpose of keeping the bottom securely in place. How you use bondage is up to you.

A person can be restrained in many ways, but all good bondage must follow these guidelines:

• The person should be restrained in a secure but

comfortable way. Most people do not want to be able to break free of the bondage. However, for some people, the illusion of restraint is enough to turn them on. In such cases, the bondage need not be so secure.

• The person's blood circulation and breathing must not be restricted. Some good rules to follow in this regard are:

· Never tie anything around the neck.

· Be careful not to tie too tightly anywhere the flow of blood might be restricted. Be especially careful at the wrists and crotch.

· When tying around the chest area, ask the person to inhale deeply and hold the breath before you secure the bondage. This way you know they have enough room to breathe comfortably while in bondage.

· Do not cover the mouth or nostrils. Breathing should be free and unobstructed. There may be cases when either the mouth or the nostrils may be covered (but not both, of course). In such cases, you must make sure that breathing is free and unobstructed. For example, if someone's nasal passages are congested, you would never want to cover their mouth. Use common sense.

· If the arms of the person in bondage are above shoulder level, realize that the blood flow is slowing to the arms and hands and that the arms will likely need to be lowered rather soon. Ask the person in

79

bondage periodically how their hands feel. If they are getting at all numb or tingly, lower the arms immediately. Other signs of arms that need to be lowered are hands that are cool to the touch or hands turning bluish in color.

· If a person is in very restrictive bondage for a long period of time they should be allowed to move their limbs somewhat during the scene. The human body maintains proper blood circulation partly through the constant pumping of blood caused by the parts of the body moving. If a body is still for a long period of time, this process can be obstructed.

· Never leave someone in bondage unattended. Even with the simplest bondage, a physical or emotional problem may arise and you should be there to attend to their needs.

• Make sure you can get anyone in bondage out of bondage quickly. In an emergency situation (not common, but possible), unrestrain the person as quickly as you can. Usually this means cutting the bondage off. Don't worry about your precious bondage gear. No gear is worth the safety of a human being. Cutlery and medical supply outlets carry a type of scissor used by nurses and doctors to cut bandages off. They have a blunt end on the bottom portion of the cutting blade. This allows the cutter to press the blunt cutting blade next to the skin and under the bandage (or rope, leather, or whatever is restraining them) without slicing the person's skin while cutting off the bondage. This type of scissor should always be available when you are playing with bondage. If you play with metal bondage, such as chains or handcuffs, a pair of heavy duty bolt cutters would certainly be handy to have around in cases of emergency.

• Do your bondage slowly. Most people prefer to be put into and taken out of bondage gradually, rather than quickly. The sensuality of bondage is enhanced when done slowly. In addition to increasing the enjoyment of the bondage, proceeding slowly allows the person doing the bondage to take plenty of time to make sure that the bondage is done safely.

A person can be restrained in many ways. Some of the methods of bondage are tying, wrapping, locking, and confining. Let's look at each of these individually.

The most common type of bondage is tying someone up, usually with rope, although many other materials can be used. Some tying bondage situations are:

· wrists tied together behind the back
· wrists and ankles, each tied together
· wrists and ankles tied in spread eagle fashion with a wrist or ankle each tied to a corner (often on a bed)
· wrists tied to thighs

A frequent mistake made when tying someone is to wrap the rope (or whatever) around the limb in such a way that when the bottom pulls on it the bondage becomes tighter. This may eventually restrict the circulation, and this should be avoided. Always make sure to tie the bondage in such a way that the bottom can pull against it (which they often will - that's part of the fun of it) without it getting tighter.

There is a great misconception that to be good at tying bondage you should know lots of different knots. Actually, most bondage enthusiasts easily get by with one secure knot. The favorite of these is the square knot. It would certainly be fun and useful to know others, but for most situations it is not at all necessary.

Apart from tying limbs, one can use rope and other similar materials to tie in other ways. A woman's breasts can be tied as can a man's genitals. Also, various kinds of body harnesses can be constructed on someone. This is usually considered a more advanced technique, but it is really not that difficult.

If someone interested in bondage were to ask where to start, I would tell them to purchase about 50-100 feet of rope and start playing. Rope is, in my opinion, by far the most versatile type of bondage gear you can have. And it's cheap and portable. Also, rope can easily be cut off someone if necessary.

Incidentally, many different kinds of rope can be used for bondage. It's pretty much a matter of taste. My preference is number 8 (1/4") braided nylon rope. This type of rope is readily available at most hardware stores and offers many advantages. It is smooth and therefore does not pose a great risk of rope burn when pulling it against the skin. Being braided and not twisted, it will not unravel in a washing machine if you decide to wash your rope. Washing your rope before you use it (to soften it) and after playing (if it came in contact with potentially dangerous body fluids) is a good idea. Also, when you cut twisted rope it unravels quickly. Braided rope does not unravel as quickly. If you wish to finish the ends of your nylon rope so they won't unravel at all, simply hold the end of the rope slightly above a flame for a few seconds.

Since nylon melts, this will melt the end of the rope. Then use a wooden stick, or similar object, to press the melted end together. Do not touch the hot nylon with your hands. It will burn you. Once the end is cool, it will not unravel.

When the entire body is wrapped in a bondage material this is called mummification. This is a special type of bondage that many people enjoy. The body is wrapped (usually in plastic food wrap, believe it or not) so that it eventually resembles an Egyptian mummy. This is a very intense form of bondage and should probably not be attempted by a complete beginner.

When wrapping the body, always make sure to leave the nose and mouth uncovered and that the breathing is not being restricted in any way. Unless the wrapping is awfully tight, there is little danger of restricting blood circulation with this type of bondage.

Since the entire body is encased, often in a nonporous material, there is some risk of the body overheating. Be careful. Keep plenty of water around. If the bottom is in a prone position have a flexible straw or rubber tube handy so they can drink without hassle.

If the wrapping material is disposable (such as the plastic wrap is), simply cut off the wrapping to release the bondage. Once again, use the special blunt end bandage scissors for this purpose. Because the temperature usually rises substantially inside a mummification bondage, release the bondage slowly so the cool flow of air is not a great shock to the person. This will increase the enjoyment of the release from bondage.

Mummification can be done with other materials besides plastic wrap. An inexpensive and comfortable mummification can be done with an old sheet. Cut some of the sheet into strips and leave the majority of the sheet intact. The body can then be wrapped tightly in the large piece of sheet and tied securely with the strips of sheeting. The advantage to this kind of wrapping material is that it is porous and can breathe, thus eliminating much overheating danger.

You can also wrap portions of the body. The most common part of the body to do this to is the head. Once again, make sure to leave the nose and mouth exposed so breathing is not restricted.

When we speak of locking kinds of bondage, we are usually referring to metal bondage. This can include chain, metal locks, handcuffs, and specially made metal bondage gear. There is very little mystery as to how to use this kind of equipment. Generally you just put it on and lock it.

The most important thing to remember in metal bondage is to make sure you have the key. There's nothing worse than putting someone in a pair of handcuffs and then discovering you can't set them free.

If you are using padlocks, consider getting a set that are all keyed to the same key. That way you know that one key opens them all. These kinds of padlocks are readily available at locksmith shops.

Another kind of locking bondage might be various wooden and leather bondage equipment. A common piece of wooden equipment is a stocks, similar to those used by the early American Puritans. Some leather wrist and ankle restraints have a locking feature. Once again, if they lock with a key, have it handy. Preferably, have a spare.

Also remember that sharps edges and corners of metal gear can be uncomfortable and possibly dangerous. If necessary, put some form of soft protection between the metal and the person.

84

Confining is placing someone inside a locked space — a sort of erotic imprisonment. This can be done in a number of ways. Putting someone in a cage will certainly confine them. But few people have a cage sitting around the house large enough for a human being. Improvise. A closet can easily form a kind of cage.

Flagellation

Anytime you strike a part of someone's body with your hand or an implement (belt, whip, paddle, riding crop, etc.), you are flagellating them. Flagellation is one of the more common types of S/M play.

Whether you're using your hand, a whip, a paddle, a belt, or whatever, the guidelines for flagellation below apply.

- Never strike:

  - directly on a bony area of the body (spine, collar bone, elbows, knee caps, shins, etc.)

  - the neck or head

  - the kidney area. This is the area on either side of the back just above the waist. The kidneys are very near the surface and can be bruised easily.

  - the back of the knees

- The most popular areas for flagellation are the buttocks and the muscled parts of the upper and middle back. However, just because these are the most popular spots

85

does not mean that everyone will enjoy being struck there. Communicate with your partner to discover their "hot" spots.

- Always start slowly and build the intensity of the blows gradually. It is a very common error for the top to strike the bottom too hard and/or too fast. Generally, the first strikes should be soft and gentle. Each succeeding strike may be progressively harder until you have reached an enjoyable level of tolerance.

- Be careful not to let what you are flagellating a person with wrap around and strike the side of the body. For example, when whipping someone's back the tips of the whip can wrap around and strike the sensitive area on either side of the torso. Few people enjoy this feeling. Work at keeping your aim precise and away from these sensitive areas.

If you are going to use something other than your hand to strike someone, practice first. Use a target such as an old pillow or a toy stuffed animal. What you're trying to do during such practice sessions is fine tune your aim. You want to make sure you hit your intended target. One inadvertent badly aimed blow can ruin a scene. Having good aim is usually not too difficult with very short or solid implements, such as a short paddle or a riding crop, but can be much more difficult with flexible whips or long rattan canes.

Flagellation is in many ways one of the easiest types of scenes to do, but it is also one of the types of scenes most frequently done incorrectly. The apparent simplicity of it can be deceiving. Once again, remember to start slowly and build gradually. Not everyone enjoys being struck with the same intensity. By starting with light strikes and building slowly, you will more easily be able to gauge the intensity your partner likes without exceeding their individual limits.

Almost anything can be used to sensually strike someone. Be creative. Some of the most common implements are whips, paddles, belts, riding crops, straps, and rattan canes. And of course, the human hand. Yes, spanking is a type of flagellation. Other common household items you can use for flagellation are hair brushes, wooden spoons, and spatulas.

Sensory Deprivation

When you restrict or eliminate someone's sensory input, you are using sensory deprivation. Blindfolding would be a type of sensory deprivation that most people are familiar with.

There is really only one guideline in regards to sensory deprivation. When you restrict or eliminate one sense (sight, hearing, touch, taste, or smell), the other senses become more acutely sensitive. For example, if you blindfold somebody, thereby eliminating their ability to see, their sensitivity to your touch will increase dramatically. The slightest touch may send sensations rushing through their body. The same touch administered while they were able to see might not have a similar effect.

The more senses you restrict or control, the more responsive the remaining senses become.

Eliminating the ability to see is the most common sensory deprivation method used. There are many ways to do this. The easiest is for the top to simply order the bottom to close their eyes until they are told to open them. If the bottom is feeling at all submissive, this usually works quite well. Blindfolds are another common way to deprive someone of their sight. A handkerchief, or any piece of cloth, can be used for this purpose. A safety note — when you put a blindfold on someone, always check first whether they wear contact lenses. If they do, you should put the blindfold on very loosely, choose a type of blindfold that does not press on the eye, or ask them to remove their contacts before you continue to play. Pressure on the contacts could cause damage to the eye. Be careful.

You can not really deprive someone of touch, but you can control what they do touch. Putting someone's hands in a pair of gloves, for example, means they can not touch and feel anything other than the inside of the gloves. Restricting the movement of their fingers reduces their ability to touch.

There are two ways to deprive hearing — eliminate hearing or control what the person hears. The safest way to eliminate someone's ability to hear is to use ear plugs. Drugstores sell a type of foam ear plug that inserts into the ear canal and effectively blocks sound. When using such ear plugs, the bottom should insert them themselves. If someone else does it there is a risk of pushing too hard and damaging the ear.

To control what the other person hears you may simply want to play a certain type of music. To eliminate all sound but the music, you could place a pair of headphones on the bottom. Now they'll only hear what music you play. If you're electronically inclined, perhaps you could hook up a microphone to the headphones so that all sound but that of your voice is eliminated. This can be very effective.

You can't really deprive smell because that would mean cutting off the nasal passages and that could introduce the risk of the bottom not getting enough air to breathe. Not a good idea. Yes, some advanced players might choose to allow a partner to breathe only through their mouth, but unless the partners are advanced and know each other well, it is usually best to leave both the nose and mouth unrestricted.

Even if you can't block someone's smell, you can control what they do smell. For someone who enjoys leather, placing some leather near them during a scene might elicit the right responses. For others, the natural odors of their partner's body are an incredible turn on. A smell, like any other sensory factor, can greatly affect the enjoyment of a scene.

You can also use one smell to mask another. For example, if your house smells like your household pet, that might not be a turn on for your partner. Burning some incense can quickly eliminate such odors and make the mood more sexual.

You really can not deprive anyone of the sense of taste. But you can control what they do taste. Perhaps the most popular taste is that of the other person's body.

Cock and Ball Play

When you are playing with a man's genitals, you are engaged in cock and ball play. All this really means is that you are concentrating your sensations on that area of the body. What you actually do to that area depends on personal preference. Bondage, light flagellation, skin sensation and clothespin techniques are just some of the possible ways you can play in this area.

89

The important thing to remember in cock and ball play is that a man's genitals are very sensitive. This might appear obvious, but you'd be surprised how many people play too roughly. Go slowly.

Anal/Vaginal Play

The main type of play one does with the anal cavity or the vagina is insertion of some object or part of the body, such as the penis, fingers or a hand. Once again, remember that these parts of the body are very sensitive areas. Be very careful when playing with them.

Some abide by the misconception that only gay men enjoy anal play. That is simply not true. Anyone, male or female, heterosexual or homosexual, may enjoy some form of anal play. The key is to proceed carefully, always remembering the delicate membranes that line the anal cavity.

While a woman's vagina usually lubricates itself to some extent, many women need additional lubrication for comfortable play in that area. And the anal cavity always needs plenty of lubrication for any kind of penetration. Always use a water-based lubricant when lubricating these areas. Drug stores carry such lubricants. Adult stores also often carry an assortment of water-based lubricants made specifically for erotic insertive play.

If you are inserting an object into a body orifice, make sure it is meant to go there. Adult erotica suppliers make a host of rubber insertion devices in a variety of shapes and sizes. Make sure that it has a wide end on it so that the object cannot accidentally slip entirely into the cavity. Many a hospital emergency room attendant has seen cases of objects inserted into rectums that the receivers were unable to retrieve without professional help. To avoid such embarrassment and inconvenience, not to mention the medical bills, be mindful of what you insert into someone and how you insert it.

Read the chapter on safety in regards to insertive play. There are a number of safety issues you should know before you engage in this type of play.

Skin Sensation

Skin sensation is a broad category of S/M play that utilizes the sensitivity of the skin. Yes, it's true that most physical S/M technique involves the sensitivity of the skin, but skin sensation scenes usually involve light, surface skin sensations. The two most common kinds of skin sensation scenes include abrasion and temperature. In addition, there is one type of abrasion technique, shaving, that is so popular it will be addressed separately.

Skin sensation scenes are usually more effective and enjoyable when a lighter touch or slow approach is used. A mild sensation doled out over a longer period of time can lead to a state of ecstasy that more heavy handed approaches make more unattainable.

Any time you rub the skin, you are engaging in abrasion. The effect abrasion has on a person depends on four factors: the implement used, the force of the touch, the speed of the approach, and the state of the senses.

Many implements can be used for abrasion. Some common ones are toothbrushes, hair brushes, and toothpicks. Anything that can be safely run across the skin for stimulation is a possible abrasion toy.

Depending on the implement used, the force of the touch needs to be paid attention to. Obviously, you can apply a very soft brush with much more force than you can a toothpick, for example. Judging the correct amount of force is paramount to ensuring good abrasion scenes. Generally, a lighter touch produces more interesting results than a harder one.

Because abrasion scenes capitalize on the sensitivity and awareness of the skin surface, heightening the sensitivity and awareness is desirable. One way to increase awareness of the skin surface is to add some sensory deprivation to your scene. For example, when you blindfold someone, the attention they pay to their other senses, including touch, increases. This can work to the benefit of an abrasion scene.

Shaving is one of the most popular forms of abrasion scenes. Many find the sensation of being shaved enjoyable. In counterpoint, control over the hair of another has great appeal for those doing the shaving. Still others enjoy the look of a smooth body. For a number of reasons, shaving is quite popular.

Almost any part of the body that has hair can be shaved. Actually, you can also shave parts of the body that do not have hair simply to enjoy the sensation of being shaved. When shaving, there are certain technical and safety guidelines to remember.

Never shave two people with the same razor blade. In this age of disposable razors and blades, that's a pretty easy requirement to meet. The type of razor most people use for shaving scenes is the traditional safety razor. You can pick up packs of such plastic disposable razors for very little cost. When you're done with the shaving scene, throw them away. You do not want to risk the possibility of passing one person's body fluids to another.

To those who fantasize about using the old style straight

razors, I must ask you to exercise caution. With a contemporary safety razor you don't run nearly the risk of a deep cut that you do with a straight razor. In addition, it is difficult to adequately decontaminate a straight razor, although they do now make straight razors with disposable blades.

If you do decide to use a straight razor for shaving, practice first. Shaving enthusiasts often recommend that one cover an inflated balloon with shaving cream as a practice surface. If you can shave all the shaving cream off the balloon without breaking it, you have the right touch to try it on a human body.

You have two possible ways to shave someone, wet or dry. A wet shave uses some moisturizing agent, usually shaving cream, to moisten the area being shaved. This can make the shaving easier by creating less drag on the skin surface. A dry shave uses no moisturizing agent. Regardless of which type of shaving you decide to do you must always do two things — shave slowly and clean the skin surface first.

Most who enjoy shaving feel that moving the blade slowly in very short strokes works best. This gives the shaver greater control, reducing nicks and cuts. When shaving, the skin surface should be cleaned before and after shaving. If skin surface bacteria, which we all have on our skin naturally, is introduced into the body through an abrasion or cut during shaving, an annoying infection may ensue. Cleaning helps eliminate this problem.

Prior to shaving, wash the skin surface to be shaved with plain soap and water. Then wipe the surface with an antibacterial agent, such as 70% rubbing alcohol. Remember to keep alcohol away from any open flames, such as lit candles. You can then proceed. Once the area is shaved, wipe any excess moisturizer off the skin and clean the area again. Using hydrogen peroxide in this step works well. Be careful of using rubbing alcohol on someone after they have been shaved. The sensitivity of the skin after shaving will often increase their susceptibility to the alcohol's stinging effect.

If you want to enjoy the sensations of shaving without actually removing any hair, try using a credit card. Yes, a credit card. If someone is blindfolded and their body is shaved with a credit card, it is very difficult to tell it's not a blade. The mental and physical sensations of shaving can be enjoyed without the loss of any hair.

Another way to stimulate the skin surface in an S/M scene is with temperature, either hot or cold. Obviously, you want to work with temperatures that are neither too hot to burn the skin nor too cold to freeze it. But there is a wide range of temperatures in between that can be a lot of fun.

The most common hot temperature scene uses hot wax from a candle. Small drops of the hot wax can be dripped on the body to produce wonderful effects. You should only use paraffin candles, by the way, not beeswax. Beeswax melts at a higher temperature than paraffin and could blister the skin.

When using hot wax, remember that the higher you hold the candle from the body, the cooler the wax becomes before it hits the skin surface. A good approach to hot wax scenes is to hold the candle very high above the body first and slowly move the candle closer until the most pleasurable temperature level is reached.

Another common mistake made when using hot wax is to pour the drops of wax on the body too quickly. Remember the S/M sensation cycle. The submissive partner must have time to assimilate the sensation they're being given. Once again, starting slowly is usually a good idea.

A good way to use cold in an S/M scene is with an ordinary ice cube. Applied to various parts of the body it can produce great sensations. Do not leave it on any one body part too long or you run the risk of freezing that area. Move the cold around.

Clothespins

This category actually includes all forms of S/M play using any kind of clipping or clamping device. Clothespins happen to be the most common type used in S/M scenes. So, even though we're talking specifically about clothespins, we are also referring to many other such devices.

The type of clothespins to use are the ones that exert pressure created by a spring. The standard clothespin, which is two pieces of wood held together by a metal spring, is easy to find and works well for such scenes.

To apply a clothespin to a person's body, simply pinch a small portion of skin with your fingers and slowly apply the clothespin. Don't rush it. By applying the clothespin slowly you can more accurately gauge the effect it has on the bottom. Virtually any part of the skin surface can have a clothespin put on it. It depends on the needs and proclivities of the players. However, be aware that some people have very tight skin. This type of skin can be difficult to use clothespins on because of the inability to find adequate folds of skin for the clothespin to hold onto. But on even the tightest of skin you can find some portion on which clothespins will work well.

A particular phenomena occurs with most people who experience clothespins. When a clothespin of light to moderate strength is on someone for a while, their body usually adjusts to that level of stimulation. Eventually it becomes a sensual awareness only. However, when that same clothespin is removed, blood rushes back into the area and the sensation spikes upwards quickly. Be prepared for this. Once the clothespin is removed, merely a light fondling of the area with your fingers will often produce excruciating results, which may, or may not, be what is desired.

You can adjust the strength of a clothespin by using a rubberband. Wrapping the rubberband around one end of a clothespin will increase its tension, while using it on the opposite end will decrease the tension. Remember, not everyone will like the same amount of pressure.

Pleasurable removal of clothespins usually means removing them slowly, one at a time. But, of course, the removal method is entirely up to the partners involved. Whatever works.

Nipple Play

Having one's nipples played with seems to be a nearly universal pleasure for both women and men. Few people don't enjoy it, at least to some extent.

I've said it before in this book, but it's worth repeating. Go slow. Few people enjoy their nipples being twisted or pinched very hard right away. They might like that level of stimulation later in the scene, but only after their nipples have had a chance to warm up a bit.

The most common ways of playing with nipples are with the fingers or with clamping devices, such as clothespins or specially made nipple clamps. All the guidelines stated in the section on clothespins apply here as well. For much play, though, the fingers do quite nicely. If you want a more sustained stimulation, some type of clamping device will do the trick.

When playing with nipples using your fingers, experiment with a range of techniques. Press softly, hard, twist lightly, brush the tips, press lightly with your nails. Each of these will produce a different sensation. You'll know if your partner's having a good time.

If you decide to apply a nipple clamp, put it on and take it off slowly. Remember also that not all nipple clamps are created equal. They range greatly in strength. Always test a clamp first before using it.

Advanced Physical S/M Techniques

This book covers many of the basic physical S/M techniques. But there are many others. Some of them can be done by someone new to S/M, but most can not. It is important for you to realize that if you are new to S/M, you should not try any of the more advanced S/M techniques unless you are taught how to do them by someone who has a great deal of experience with S/M.

The four advanced techniques I am specifically referring to in this section are piercing, cutting, electricity, and breath control. If you are unfamiliar with these types of S/M play, refer to the glossary at the rear of this book. Most people interested in S/M do not engage in these activities at all. But if you do, it is very important for you to realize the potential dangers.

If at some point you become interested in these activities in the course of your S/M play, exercise extreme caution.

97

Never try any of them unless you have done a great deal of research and utilized the assistance of a person, or preferably more than one person, with knowledge and experience in that area. The only way to find such people is to become well networked within the S/M community. Join a responsible S/M organization. Many of these have educational programs that will teach you about these aspects of S/M.

These advanced S/M techniques, if done correctly by someone with lots of knowledge and experience, can be fun and perfectly safe. If done incorrectly, they pose a potential danger, possibly life threatening, that must be respected. You would never go sky diving without the proper training. It is just so with certain types of S/M play.

Chapter 7

THE PLAYGROUND
OF THE MIND

When most people discuss how to do S/M, they generally concentrate on the physical aspects — how to tie someone up, how to spank someone properly, how to do a hot wax scene, etc. But that's only one component of S/M. The really important part is the mind. How do you feel during an S/M scene? What goes through your mind as a scene is taking place? What we're referring to here is mental technique.

Mental technique covers the erotic world of the mind. It focuses on techniques used to enhance a person's mental enjoyment of the scene apart from the physical sensations. Mental technique is much harder to define or illustrate because it is so unique to each individual and each different scene. It is also important to remember that the physical and mental aspects of an S/M scene often, if not usually, blend one into the other in such a way that they become barely distinguishable.

What follows is a discussion of how the mind plays such an important part in S/M and how to make the best use of this fact. The discussion will give you a better idea as to how to utilize your own mental techniques to better your scenes.

The Unlimited Mind

We all have physical limitations. But our minds know no such limitations. We can think about anything without regard for physical boundaries. This fact can be exploited to both partners' benefit in an S/M scene.

Now, this is a very important concept, so pay attention. In S/M, it makes absolutely no difference what the body is doing so long as the mind is having a good time. In fact, you can experience and enjoy an S/M scene without your body being involved in any way. S/M fantasies are a good example of this. The scenes that exist in your fantasies are just as much an S/M experience as any other. This doesn't mean that most of us don't want to also experience S/M in the physical world as well. However, it is important not to dismiss your fantasies as unreal. They make you feel good and nothing that does that can be considered unreal.

Think about how important this is. You don't actually have to do something to experience the fun of that activity. Let's say you have repeatedly fantasized about being tied up and spanked severely, but the actual reality of it doesn't appeal to you much. If you can find a partner who would enjoy making you feel as though you are being tied up and spanked, you can have just as much fun with this type of scene as someone who is actually doing it. At some level, this phenomenon is utilized by everyone who enjoys S/M.

People who enjoy kidnap S/M scenes are not actually being kidnapped, but they feel that way during the scene. Their mind, at least to some extent, believes they are being kidnapped. People who enjoy being tortured by their captor would not necessarily enjoy being tortured in reality, but they feel that way during a scene. People who enjoy being a slave to a master or mistress might not actually be

100

slaves, but they feel that way during the scene.

In order for someone to enjoy the mental aspect of S/M, they must be able to tap into the childlike quality of imaginative play. In other words, they must be able to pretend. Now, there may be some in the S/M community who will balk at using the term pretend. "But what we do is real," many will say. Yes, it is real, but it is also in the realm of make believe.

And therein lies the dilemma many face in S/M — how to make a scene real enough to be exciting, but grounded enough in reality so as to abide by the safe, sane and consensual guidelines. The satisfactory solving of this dilemma is the goal of mental S/M technique.

The Reality Threshold

Each S/M player has what I call a reality threshold. This threshold is the degree of reality they find necessary to enjoy an S/M scene. In other words, how much of the S/M situation must be based in reality for there to be a successful S/M experience? Some find they need little of a scene based in reality while others find it very necessary. No two people are the same.

Finding a person's reality threshold is an inexact art form, at best. There is no one method of getting this information. One good reason for this is that the person you are playing with, and probably you yourself, have not given this much thought. You know what turns you on, but you have not broken it down into reality and fantasy components. And perhaps there is no need to. Sometimes excessive analysis of something ruins the enjoyment of it.

But extensive analysis is not necessary here. Simply having a sense of a person's reality threshold is all that is necessary. It is more something you will feel about a person than a fact you can know.

Generally, the lower a person's reality threshold, the easier it is for them to realize their S/M fantasies. The reason is obvious. Their mind can more easily fill in the reality gaps. While one person might need a fully equipped dungeon with lots of ornate S/M gear and a partner who maintains a strict role persona, another person might only need a dimly lit bedroom with a few S/M toys and a partner who maintains some semblance of the S/M role they are playing. Neither way is more correct, but the latter person is going to find it a lot easier to get their S/M needs met.

Getting the Information You Need

In order for your mental technique to be productive, you must have a pretty good idea of what turns your partner on. In the negotiation process outlined earlier in this book, you will get much of this information. Unfortunately, though, negotiations often become merely a listing of physical dos and don'ts. Many mental requirements important to a scene are often left unsaid.

Two people might both enjoy spanking, for example. One partner might think of spanking as a fantasy punishment scene, while the other considers spanking as merely serving their partner's dominant or submissive needs. Spanking means something different to each of these people. You might have gotten an "I like spanking" from them during the negotiations, but that doesn't tell you how they like it administered or what situation the fantasy represents.

It would be nice if there were some magic way to get

such information, but there isn't. It must be done on a case by case basis. But it must be done if your scenes are to reach the heights of pleasure you desire.

Good, honest and open communication between partners is vital. Tell your partner exactly how you feel about S/M and what situations turn you on. What mental and emotional elements are required for the scene to work for you? Do you like an extremely affectionate or rigid approach from your partner? What erotic fantasies do you dream about and hope to have fulfilled in reality? And how much of this should remain fantasy? Expect such information from your partner also. You have as much right to this information as you do to their safer sex guidelines and safe words. You are 50% of the scene. Besides, if you don't get this information you are likely to have a not so memorable scene anyway. So why bother? Go into the scene with as much preparation as possible.

Mind Before Body

Before you ever had sex, your mind may have enjoyed countless sexual experiences in your fantasies. Before you experience anything in life, you usually think about it first. So it is with S/M.

No two people take the same path to S/M. But one thing is almost always true. Their mind usually thought about it before they did it with their body. And usually it takes time to get around to trying any new idea out. Few people think about something as exciting as S/M one day and do it the next. They dwell on it for a while.

Using the mind-before-body concept can be a useful tool for S/M play. If you have an interest in some aspect of S/M and your partner currently does not, or has never thought about it before, introduce the idea in a non-threatening way, perhaps in a casual conversation. Or leave a magazine or book around the house which discusses the S/M activity you want to experiment with. Or introduce the idea during your other erotic play without acting on it. If your partner has an inclination toward such an S/M activity, their mind will dwell on it and eventually they may decide they want to try it. Allowing plenty of time to let it simmer is the key. Of course, they just might not have any interest at all in what you brought up and that's OK too. There are plenty of other choices in S/M.

The Power of the Voice

The power of the human voice is amazing. A few well-chosen words delivered with the right volume, pace and inflection can influence someone greatly in a matter of seconds. This holds true for one's sexuality as well.

Learn to use your voice to your advantage in S/M scenes. Experiment with the words you use and how you deliver them. Experiment with moments of silence as a counterpoint to the sound of your voice. Someone gifted verbally can take their partner through the most amazing scenes while doing nothing more, physically, than holding that person. The voice influences the mind and it can take off for erotic outer space searching for undiscovered territory. Remember also that how you say something often is more important than what you say.

Roles

Role play is a vital part of much of S/M. Some people do not have a complete S/M experience unless a certain amount of role play takes place. Although various roles might manifest themselves in certain physical ways, role play is basically a mental S/M technique.

What is a role? A role is the part you play in the erotic theater presentation we call a scene. It is the personality you adopt for the duration of the scene. The term "role" is also sometimes used to identify the side of the power dynamics you are playing on. For example, the bottom role or top role, the dominant role or the submissive role.

Roles can be based in either reality or fantasy. The role of nurse or doctor is a role based in reality. Nurses and doctors really do exist, while an Amazon queen is more of a fantasy role — although I guess perhaps some such person existed in another place and time.

The degree of submersion into the role can also vary from person to person. While one person may elect to take on only a few of the characteristics of a role, another may try to literally become that role with costuming, voice, character, personality and manner, all in line with the assumption of that role. There is no one right way to play.

The S/M community tends to foster a number of traditional S/M play roles. This does not mean these are the best ones. They are simply the roles that a large percentage of the S/M population favors. Just a few of the more popular are master/mistress-slave, father/mother-son/daughter, abductor-captor, and dungeon master/mistress-torture victim. You will encounter such roles if you develop a network within the S/M community. Be careful not to be too heavily influenced by other people's preferences. If the roles you prefer to play with do not fall within the traditional styles, do not try to conform. Being open to experiencing new things is always a good idea, but bending your desires solely to meet the

105

approval of others rarely proves to be worthwhile. Be your own person. Play your own way.

I would venture to say that most people in the S/M scene do not play with specific roles. Rather, the roles they adopt are personal creations pieced together from various elements of different roles they fantasize about or encounter in daily life. Since they are personal creations, they can be fulfilling erotically because more is invested in them.

Chapter 8

S/M GEAR

When someone unfamiliar with S/M hears it mentioned, they might say "Oh, you like all that whips and chains stuff." They equate S/M with S/M gear (also called S/M toys or S/M equipment), though they are not the same at all. But many people who enjoy S/M do like to use certain kinds of gear to enhance their play. That's what we'll talk about here.

First, let's dispel some misconceptions about S/M gear. Here are three very common ones.

- S/M gear is expensive.
- S/M gear is difficult to use. It takes a lot of experience to use them properly.
- S/M gear can only be purchased at specialty S/M retail outlets.

None of these are true.

S/M gear is not necessarily expensive. Yes, if you want to dress in lots of expensive leather clothing, play in an elaborately equipped playspace and have every conceivable S/M toy on the market, you're going to spend a lot of money. But few people do this. And there's no need to.

Much of the gear one uses in S/M is fairly easy to use and the newcomer can feel comfortable using it right away. Of course, some gear does take more knowledge and experience to use properly.

And yes, S/M gear is often purchased at specialty S/M retail outlets, but that's not the only place S/M gear can be found.

Buying S/M Gear

There are a number of S/M gear retailers throughout the United States and Europe that specialize in supplying S/M aficionados equipment to help them fulfill their fantasies. These retailers fall into three distinct categories: retail store, mail order vendor, or small specialty provider.

Retail stores that specialize in S/M gear tend to do business in the larger urban centers. If you live in a large city, there is likely one near you. Some stores, such as adult erotica stores, sell some S/M gear as part of the array of adult items they stock.

Mail order vendors offer an opportunity for anyone to buy S/M gear, no matter where they live. Some of these companies specialize in only certain types of S/M gear — bondage, for example — while others offer a vast array of items to choose from. While retail stores provide the shopper an opportunity to actually see and scrutinize the item being purchased, mail order often provides a price incentive. Shop around. Either option can provide you with excellent equipment at a good price.

Be aware of the possibility that laws in your area may not allow certain types of S/M or erotic materials to be sent through the mail.

Another type of S/M gear provider is the small specialty provider. This is often a one-person business operation that makes and sells S/M gear. This person might make custom leather clothing, unique S/M gear, or high quality whips. Whatever they make, they can offer personal service and fine-quality items due to their personal attention to your needs. These specialty providers are best sought out by the personal referral of others in the S/M community.

Wherever you buy S/M gear, buy judiciously. Decide if it's something you'll really use. Don't buy something you have no interest in just because you think it's something you should have. Pay attention to quality. S/M gear quality varies greatly. It's hard to describe what is meant here by quality, but, just as with other items you purchase, you'll know it when you see it.

Many mail order vendors illustrate how an item is used in their catalogs. But if you come across an item in a store and you're not sure how it's used, ask. Believe me, clerks in such stores have heard it all. There's nothing you can ask that will shock them. Besides, they are there to help you.

Preparing a Playspace

In addition to purchasing some S/M gear, you might also wish to prepare a place in your home to play. Some people choose to set aside a separate area of their living space exclusively for S/M play. For most, though, that is not practical. Using a bedroom or guestroom is sufficient. And remember, S/M can take place anywhere. Use your imagination.

Consider how soundproof your play space is. Could your neighbors hear you if the play got a little loud? What room you decide to use might depend on this factor. If you have children or other people living with you, can the room be made private and secure? You don't want unexpected visitors popping in during your scene.

Variable lighting might be a nice addition. If you and your partner have a particular setting you enjoy for your fantasies, medical or military, for example, can your space be made to look somewhat like those settings easily? A few white sheets hung as separators along with a few medical instruments could easily give the indication of a medical setting. An army cot and some army gear could create a military setting. Of course, if your reality threshold is low and you can just as well imagine all these things and enjoy the scene just as much, then so much the better for you.

One very handy thing to install in your playspace is a set of secure eye bolts. These can be screwed or bolted into place and provide excellent grounding points for bondage. When installing these bolts, always make sure they are strong enough to hold the human weight they are intended to support. Consult a construction specialist or a friend who knows about such things. If you are uncomfortable having such eye bolts visible, hide them in inconspicuous places or, if they are visible, tell visitors they're for hanging plants.

The Inexpensive Toy Collection

Most physical S/M can be done with items you probably already have around the house. If you don't have them, they can usually be purchased in such places as grocery stores, drugstores and hardware stores. You probably have a lot of S/M toys already in your home. You've just never looked at them that way before. Although it can be a lot of fun to have more expensive S/M gear, it's not necessary, certainly not for someone just learning about S/M.

110

Next time you're in a drugstore, start looking at the items sold there from a different viewpoint. A toothbrush becomes a toy to erotically tease someone's nipples. Clothesline becomes versatile bondage gear. A sleep mask becomes a comfortable blindfold. Clothespins become erotic clamping devices for nipples and other parts of the body. Leather shoe laces can be tied together to form a simple whip. Candles can be used to drop hot wax on your partner's body. You get the idea.

For little money you can buy all the gear necessary to use in the more basic S/M scenes. Below is a listing of inexpensive items that can form the foundation for a basic S/M toy collection. Over time you may want to add to the collection as your interests become more clear. But this is a good place to start. Let your creative mind lead you and I'm sure you'll add many more fun and interesting items to this list soon.

• Rope

Rope is the most versatile bondage gear you can have. With just 50 to 100 feet of rope you can create countless bondage situations to delight you and your partner. Strands of the rope can also be tied together to form a makeshift whip. Rope of some kind is always available in hardware stores and often available in grocery and drugstores.

• Large square of cloth

If you have a fabric store nearby, try to buy a scrap of thin, linen fabric about 3 feet square. Darker colors work better. If you don't have such fabric handy, a

111

very large handkerchief will do just fine. Or you can cut up an old sheet. This can be used in many ways. Folded flat and tied around the eyes it serves as a blindfold. Open it up and cover the entire head and it becomes a type of hood. You don't have to worry about disrupting someone's breathing because they can breathe easily through the fabric (check this out first). Rolled thin and tied around the mouth it becomes a gag. Rolled thick it can be used to beat your partner with in a very sensual way. This is fun for both partners. It allows the top to have the sensation of hitting the bottom very hard. The bottom can also have the sensation of being truly beaten, even though the fabric is so soft it delivers only a mild thudding sensation.

Since linen fabric is usually thin enough to let light pass through, one layer will disrupt a bottom's vision, but not completely block it off. This may be desirable with someone leery of being blindfolded, but wanting to experiment with it. When you fold the fabric to form two layers, it becomes opaque and blocks out all light.

- Belt

A simple leather belt makes an excellent flagellating device. Remember to never hit anyone with the buckle portion of a belt.

- Candles

Paraffin candles can be used to drip hot wax on your partner.

- Leather shoe laces

  Leather rawhide shoe laces can be used for certain kinds of bondage and also tied together to form a small, simple whip.

- Plastic wrap

  Plastic food wrap can be used as an alternative bondage device instead of rope. Wrap the plastic around the parts of the body you wish to restrain a few times and you'll be surprised how strong and secure it is. To remove, just cut it. It's cheap. If you wrap it around the head you can form a tight fitting hood. Remember to never cover the mouth or the nose with such a hood. When removing plastic wrap from the head area by cutting it off, be very careful and stay away from the eye area. Use only the bandage scissors suggested.

- Duct Tape

  This type of tape is very useful for bondage. Never apply it directly to the skin. Cover the area first. Plastic wrap works well for this. Plastic wrap wrapped around the eyes and then covered with duct tape forms a great blindfold. Remember you will have to cut this type of bondage off someone. But tape is relatively cheap.

- Bandage scissors

  In the interest of safety, it is a good idea to have a pair of these in your collection in case you need to get someone out of bondage quickly. They cost only a few dollars and are available at medical supply and some cutlery stores.

- Clothespins

Clothespins can be used as clamping devices for the nipples, as well as other parts of the body. Wooden clothespins with spring action are the ones you want.

- Chop sticks

Next time you go to a Chinese restaurant, ask if you can keep the chop sticks. They make excellent tapping devices. Of course, you can also buy them in many grocery stores. A constant series of light tapping on certain parts of the body can become excruciatingly delightful.

- Toothbrush

A toothbrush is an excellent abrasion device for all parts of the body, including the nipples. If you get the kind with the pointed rubber tip on the end, this can also be used to tease and delight.

- Safer sex items

No toy collection would be complete without those things to make any sex you might have safer. These include condoms, latex exam gloves, dental dams, and water-based lubricant. Look to the chapter on safety for more specifics about safer sex.

With the items listed above you can do bondage scenes, flagellation scenes, cock and ball play, anal/vaginal play, nipple play, abrasion scenes, temperature scenes, and sensory deprivation scenes, to name just a few. One of the joys in working with common, everyday objects in your S/M play is that it engages your brain in a way that ready-made S/M gear often does not. If you buy a pair of leather wrist restraints, you know what they do and how to use them. But a simple length of rope offers your mind endless bondage possibilities. You become intimately involved in the use of the equipment and that often makes the scene more satisfying.

Traveling With S/M Gear

If you travel and wish to bring some S/M gear with you, there are certain considerations you should think about. Traveling across a foreign border can often pose a risk because you may be unfamiliar with laws regarding such items. When traveling abroad, it is often a good idea to keep your S/M gear simple and inconspicuous. A length of rope and clothespins is to hang your hand-washed clothes up in your hotel room, right? And a belt is something you would have anyway. A toothbrush, handkerchief, and leather shoe laces are certainly items anyone might have with them on a trip.

Space is also a consideration. Packing bulky S/M gear can take up valuable space in your luggage. With a little thought and planning, you can pack plenty of S/M gear to enjoy yourself while not weighing you down unnecessarily.

If you do decide to bring S/M gear that will likely be perceived as such, never take it on the plane with you. Airlines have strict regulations about what can be brought on a plane. Some S/M gear can be seen as a potential weapon and airline officials will not allow them in the passenger area. Just to be sure, check these items in your baggage. If you are travelling within the United States, for example, and check your baggage, very few things would cause alarm to airline officials. They are a lot more concerned with bombs than they are with your sexual lifestyle.

Also remember to pack safe sex items. Having these items always handy will ensure that you will not be tempted to engage in unsafe behavior. Be prepared.

Chapter 9

FINDING S/M PARTNERS

All the information in this book won't do you much good if you don't have a partner to play with. Finding a compatible partner without the S/M component can be difficult enough. Adding S/M to the equation can complicate matters. But meeting others interested in S/M is not as difficult as you might imagine.

Let's examine some ways you can find S/M partners.

Organizations and Clubs

There are now S/M support, educational and social organizations and clubs in virtually every large urban area of the United States. Similar groups are springing up in other parts of the world. These groups provide one of the best forums to meet others. They also often offer you the benefit of learning more about S/M in the process. Many S/M organizations provide educational events as part of their activities. They meet to discuss and/or demonstrate S/M play. This offers you an opportunity to expand your S/M skills and increase your fantasy options.

Becoming involved in one of the S/M organizations or clubs is one of the most direct, and safest, ways to meet others who share your interest in safe, sane and consensual S/M play.

Personals Advertising

Advertising for partners in a publication no longer holds the same societal stigma it once did. Some of the most respected magazines now feature personal classified advertising sections.

Closely examine some of the personal ads that appear in the magazines you are considering placing your ad in. Study them carefully. How are they worded? What abbreviations do they use? Which ads appeal to you? What ads turn you off? Others will probably react to such ads the same way you do. You want your ad to be a turn on and to attract the right kind of play partner, don't you? Then take the time to study such ads so you can tailor yours to better suit your needs. Here are a few tips on wording your ad:

- Do not use your home phone number or address in your ad. Most people who respond will be courteous, but every now and then someone will call you at a ridiculous hour of the day, or worse yet, they might just drop by if you use your home address. Not a good idea. Post office boxes or mail drop services are good alternatives for a mailing address. A computerized voice mail answering service can assign you a phone number that you can place in your ad. Anyone can then leave you a message, in their own words, any time of day or night without disturbing you. It's probably not a good idea to use an answering service with live operators since some of your respondents might be intimidated due to the subject matter of their call. Some publications offer a mail box service to their classified advertisers. You list the publication's box number and the publication will forward your mail to you.

- Be honest. Do not lie in your ad. If you describe yourself, be accurate. If you are looking for a specific kind of person, say so. If you list S/M activities in your ad that you enjoy, make sure that you do enjoy them. If you are a newcomer to S/M, do not pretend to be experienced. Dishonesty in a personals ad can lead to an unsatisfactory experience for both partners.

- Be clear about what is reality and what is fantasy. Do not say in your ad that you love to be beaten hard or tied up for hours unless that is really what you like. Perhaps what you really like is the fantasy of being beaten hard and tied up for hours, but not the reality. Make the distinction clear in your ad. Someone reading your ad only has your words to assess you by.

- Do not limit your options. When writing personal ads, people are often too specific. For example, putting a narrow age requirement in your ad means that people who do not fall into that range will not contact you. If you said you were looking for people between the ages of 30 and 32, then the person who is 33 (and possibly just the right partner for you) will not answer your ad. Wouldn't that be a shame?

- Title your ad. Some magazines and newspapers offer short titles in their personals advertising. If you have this option, take advantage of it. An ad with a short, interesting title is more likely to be noticed than one without it.

- Realize that listing a mailing address rather than a phone number will probably reduce the number of responses you get from your ad. People are generally much more likely to place a phone call than write a letter. Also, requesting a photo to be mailed might reduce your responses. Some people are uneasy about sending their photo in the mail. You must weigh the means of contact with the probable outcome. A greater number of responses is not necessarily the goal; what you want is a good S/M experience. After all, all it takes is just one good response.

- Depending on the publication, you may have to compose the ad in a more subtle style. If you are placing an ad in a mainstream publication, rather than one targeted at the S/M, or S/M friendly, community, you may need to use wording that indicates your interests without being too obvious. You might want to say "a woman with a dominant personality" rather than "a leather clad dominatrix with whip in hand" or "a man with a desire to serve" rather than "a male slave who craves to kiss your feet."

S/M-Related Events

As the S/M community grows, so do opportunities to meet others who share such interests. There are a number of S/M-related events that take place throughout the United States, Canada and Europe. Some of these cater to people of a particular sex or sexual orientation, while others can be enjoyed by anyone interested in the scene.

These events include dances, workshops, art shows, contests, discussion groups, play parties, and travel excursions, to name a few. Meeting others interested in S/M in a variety of settings like these is an opportunity that should be taken advantage of.

It is not possible to list all such events in this book. Using the many resources available in the community is the way to find out about them. Some will be local, while others require travel.

Computer Bulletin Boards

With the personal computer quickly becoming a fixture in many homes, meeting people via computer hookup seemed an inevitability. There are now many different kinds of computer bulletin boards where people with similar interests can communicate with each other.

With the use of these services people correspond, swap information and insights, even arrange to meet each other if they appear compatible. S/M dating has entered the computer age.

The basic requirements are that you have at your disposal a personal computer, a modem, and telecommunications software. If you are unfamiliar with using these bulletin boards, there are excellent books available on the subject.

Bars

Unless you're a gay man, bars will not offer you much of an opportunity for meeting potential partners. In some large urban areas there are a few night spots where men and women of all orientations can meet others with similar S/M interests, but these clubs are few in number.

If you are a gay man, however, gay leather bars do

offer an opportunity to meet others into S/M. Not everyone who frequents a leather bar is necessarily into S/M, though many are.

Although how you dress is entirely up to you, if you plan on going to a leather bar you will probably feel more comfortable dressing to fit in. Leather bars are generally becoming more accepting of a wide range of dress, but leather or "butch" attire will allow you to fit in better. Leather wear can be as simple as a leather vest with jeans and boots. If you don't wish to wear leather, a simple dark t-shirt with jeans and work boots will suffice.

I am not personally in favor of leather dress codes in bars because I would rather have kinky people of all kinds there rather than people who just happen to be wearing leather. Yes, wearing leather can certainly indicate a fetish interest in leather. And that's great. But dressing in leather is by no means a certain indication of an interest in S/M. However, the reality is that many leather bars do have dress codes and probably always will. If you have doubts about what to wear to a particular bar, call them up. Most bartenders will gladly give you their preferred dress code.

When meeting someone in a bar, your screening of potential partners needs to be particularly thorough. In this situation you will probably not have the advantage of asking anyone else if they have information about this person. Asking for a phone number and talking later will give you more time to get to know them and is generally good advice. If you do decide to go home with someone directly from a bar, make sure the person has not been drinking heavily and is not under the influence of any drugs. If they are, don't leave with them. It would most likely not be a very good experience anyway and it could be dangerous. Wait till another time when you are both in control of all faculties.

Referrals

Meeting someone by referral is one of the best ways to connect with S/M partners. It has these distinct advantages:

- You know the person referring and, hopefully, trust their judgment as to the other person's character and trustworthiness.

- You know already that the person is interested in some of the same kinds of erotic play you are.

- You can ask the person referring you questions about the person and therefore have some third-party information about the potential playmate.

Yes, I know this smacks of being a blind date, but lots of blind dates have resulted in wonderful relationships. Give it a chance.

Approaching the Subject in a Non-S/M Setting

There are ways to approach the subject of S/M in non-S/M settings. A subtle approach is usually best. Here are some ways to find out if someone might be interested in S/M.

- If you are already dating someone, mention some relatively non-threatening S/M activity as part of your "hot talk" during your lovemaking. If those ideas appear to turn your partner on, proceed to investigate further. Go slowly. Don't assume that because someone shows an interest in S/M they necessarily want to dive right in. Most people new to S/M require a lot of time to become comfortable with the idea. Be patient.

- Wear some subtle indication of your S/M interest. For example, I have seen small lapel pins in the shape of handcuffs. Wearing such a pin on your clothing will likely indicate to someone interested in S/M that you might be interested too. Of course, others who see the pin will probably just consider it a trendy fashion statement. Be creative.

- Slipping some S/M scene buzzwords into a conversation can clue the other person in on your interests. For example, the statement "the beauty of your eyes makes me want to *submit* to you completely" means two very different things depending on whether you find S/M exciting or not.

Many of the resources that might be helpful in meeting others are listed in The S/M Resource Guide. See the section at the end of the book for details.

Chapter 10

TIPS

This chapter includes a variety of tips that will hopefully increase the enjoyment of your S/M play.

The Importance Of Communication

Ask any psychotherapist or counselor what is wrong with bad relationships and they'll say — lack of communication. This if often the case with S/M scenes that go awry.

Although it has been stressed in this book before, it bears repeating: communicate with your partner. Your partner is not a mind reader and neither are you. Be open about your desires, fantasies and needs and expect the same of your partner.

Pacing Your Scenes

Often the newcomer to S/M believes, consciously or subconsciously, that if they play at a fast pace it will appear as though they are experienced and know what they are doing. This is wrong. In fact, the opposite is true. Playing at too fast a pace is usually the sure sign of a novice.

When you play at a fast pace, you often ignore the signals your partner is giving you. If you're not responding correctly to your partner, the scene is destined to be unsatisfactory and perhaps dangerous. Take your time and pay attention to your partner. Look at their body language. Listen to what they say, even if it is only a grunt or a moan. Pace your scene according to that information.

After a Scene

When a scene is over and you are both coming down from the experience, try to stay connected for a while. S/M is an intimate activity. You are sharing powerful feelings and emotions. Disconnecting too quickly can be disconcerting. Holding each other, talking, going out to dinner, or sleeping together are all ways to stay connected after a scene.

Another good idea is to call someone the next day after a scene, particularly if it was your first scene together or if one or both partners are new to S/M. This will allow partners to process any issues left unresolved from the day before.

Avoid Ruts

When partners discover certain types of S/M play that work well for them, they often stick to those types of play exclusively. Boredom can result.

S/M offers people such a vast range of choices for play that trying new scenes is easy. Try not to get in a rut with your S/M play. At the very least, try new variations of what you already know you enjoy. For example, if you and your partner like whipping and you always whip your partner while standing, try doing it while they are lying down. Or try whipping them with different implements, various rhythms, or on different parts of the body.

Avoid Drugs

Drugs (including alcohol) do not mix well with S/M. When one is under the influence of a substance, judgment is often impaired. Safety and sanity go right out the window. I personally believe drugs and alcohol should be avoided when playing, although I'm sure some may disagree. But few would disagree that using drugs or alcohol to excess does not make for safe, or fun, S/M scenes.

Don't Play Beyond Your Abilities

Once someone has a few successful scenes they can become very sure of themselves. If this self-assuredness becomes too overblown the person may begin to consider playing with types of S/M scenes they are not yet qualified to attempt.

Realize this very moment that no one in the S/M community knows it all. There is not a single person walking the earth who is 100 percent qualified to do every kind of S/M scene possible. It is no embarrassment to admit you need to learn more about a particular type of technique. In fact, it is a sign of a good S/M player. Someone who tries to do a scene they are not yet qualified to do is an obvious novice. Experienced practitioners know this and will avoid such people.

Take the time to learn what you need to know. Ask for assistance from others in the S/M community.

Think With Your Head

This ties in with the last section about playing over your head. There may be times when the passion and excitement of a scene become so great that you are no longer thinking with your head, but with your genitals. This is very dangerous if the activity you are doing at the moment has any risks associated with it.

Be aware that this might happen and stop yourself for a moment if it does. Ask yourself if this is the wise thing to be doing. Are you qualified to do this? Is the other person qualified? Will you regret this later?

Change Play Environments

The environment you play in will often dictate the kind of scene you do. A scene done in your own bedroom will be different from one done in a hotel room. And the variety of environments can differ greatly.

By changing play environments you change the kind of scene you have. This adds variety to your play and keeps it fresh and new.

S/M In An Ongoing Relationship

S/M can be part of an ongoing relationship. It is often best that way. But long-term relationships pose a set of difficulties in regards to S/M.

The difficulties usually arise when the partners in the relationship can no longer allow themselves to share their fantasies because they fear judgment of the one they love and care for. Consciously or unconsciously, they fear that their fantasies and erotic needs will be deemed silly or wrong by their partner.

Is there an easy solution to this dilemma? No. Honest and open communication is the best solution. Merely acknowledging that this problem sometimes occurs in relationships is a large step in the right direction.

If you cannot work this out without help, get some. Find an S/M-friendly therapist or counselor and have them work with the two of you to iron out the problem.

Also remember that a certain amount of leveling off of sexual activity is normal after a couple has been together for a while. Expect this to happen.

Staying In Shape

This might seem a strange thing to be talking about in an S/M book, but it can be important. The reality is that people are usually attracted to others who are in good shape and take care of themselves. Yes, there are some who crave partners who are overweight or unkempt, but I believe they are the minority.

All the good technique and S/M gear might be of no use if your partner does not find you attractive. A little bit of exercise, good diet and proper grooming is good advice for most of us.

Chapter 11

SAFETY

Safety has been stressed throughout this book, but I feel it is important to devote an entire chapter to specifics.

S/M, like nearly every human activity, has its risks. The important thing to realize is that you can greatly minimize or eliminate those risks. This chapter will discuss how to maintain the "safe" in safe, sane, consensual and fun.

There are three types of safety we need to discuss. The first is health safety. This addresses issues regarding disease transmission between partners and how to minimize that possibility. The next is physical safety, apart from diseases. Avoiding physical damage to the body is what physical safety is all about. And finally, there's emotional safety. When you're dealing with any relationship, the importance of not damaging someone emotionally is always an issue. In S/M, with the strong power dynamics involved, emotional safety is that much more important.

Health Safety

A great deal of attention has been given lately to the risk of contracting the HIV virus, the virus responsible for Acquired Immune Deficiency Syndrome (AIDS). And that's as it should be. The HIV crisis is a serious one and any sexually active person must learn the precautions necessary to avoid contracting HIV. Luckily, avoiding contact with HIV is quite simple, as is explained below.

In addition to the HIV virus, there are many other sexually transmitted diseases that one can come in contact with. Generally, if you take adequate precautions to avoid the HIV virus you will also be avoiding a host of other sexually transmitted diseases as well. The means of avoiding them are all basically similar.

One of the joys of S/M is that so much of what you can do is virtually 100% safe as far as disease transmission goes. But some erotic practices do have a degree of risk involved. For example, when having intercourse you should use a condom. However, condoms are man made objects and, therefore, are not perfect. And not all condoms are created equal. Some are stronger and more reliable than others. In others words, a condom can fail. Often the failure of a condom is due to it being misused during intercourse, not product error. But it can happen.

Because of the various levels of risk involved in sexual activity, most safe sex educational organizations list erotic activities according to their degree of safety. That way, partners can make a more intelligent decision as to the level of safety they are willing to demand in their erotic play. To print one of these lists here might be misleading. Specific safe sex guidelines can differ amongst the various organizations.

Before deciding upon your own safe sex guidelines, get current information. There are a number of AIDS (HIV) educational organizations. There is probably one in your area. Check your local phone book. If you don't find one, call directory assistance and ask them. If you need to, call a doctor's office and get a number from them. Don't give up until you contact one.

Many of these organizations have hotlines you can call

to ask questions. See if they'll also send you some information about safe sex guidelines. Most will be happy to. That's what they are there for, after all.

These organizations were formed to educate people how to avoid contact with the HIV virus, but as was said before, if you avoid contact with HIV you generally avoid most other sexually transmitted diseases as well.

Also, it should be pointed out that there is another way to be safe. That is to play only within a monogamous relationship in which both partners have discussed their health situations with a doctor and the doctor has concluded that it is safe for them to have unprotected sex. Be cautious. Be very sure both you and your partner have consulted a doctor before engaging in unprotected sex. Also, be sure the doctor you consult is well versed in HIV and other sexually transmitted diseases. If you have any doubts, play safely until you can be sure.

When you are going to play with someone for the first time, I believe you must discuss each other's safe sex guidelines. Two people may have the same safe sex information, but the level of risk each is willing to undertake may differ.

If your potential partner is not knowledgeable about safe sex practices, it is your duty to educate them with all the knowledge you have and, if necessary, to refer them to an appropriate organization or agency that can give them further information. We must look out for each other within the S/M community, and the world at large, and educating others about safe sex practices is an important way to do so.

Sometimes talking about safe sex guidelines can be tough. Perhaps if you each write them down on a piece of paper and exchange them, it will be easier to talk about.

133

However you do it, the point is that you and your partner must enter into your erotic scenes with a full understanding of each other's safe sex guidelines.

If for some reason you do not have a chance to discuss each other's safe sex guidelines before playing, always play on the conservative side of safety. That way you are not likely to encroach on another person's safe sex rules.

The guidelines below conform to the generally accepted requirements for avoiding contact with HIV and other sexually transmitted diseases.

- If you are going to insert a part of one person's body into the orifice of another person's body, cover the inserting area with a latex barrier.

For example, during intercourse (vaginal or anal), always use a condom. The condom should be made of latex. Natural substance condoms, such as lambskin, have not proven to be good protection from the HIV virus.

Make sure to use a condom properly. Here are some tips. With the penis hard, squeeze the air out of the tip after you put it on, before you unroll it. While unrolling the condom on your penis, hold the tip. If using an unlubricated condom, lubricate it. Never use oil-based lubricants such as hand lotion or petroleum jelly. Use only water-based lubricants. These are available at drug stores. Specially made water-based sexual lubricants are also available at adult retail outlets. If you decide to ejaculate inside the condom while still inside your partner, hold the base of the condom as you pull out. However, it is always safer to pull out before ejaculating. Of course, you should never reuse a condom.

Not all condoms are manufactured with the same quality. Consult with an AIDS (HIV) education organization. They might be able to give you a list of the brands of condoms that have passed stringent studies with high marks.

If you are going to insert your fingers or hand into the vagina or anal cavity of your partner, cover it with a latex glove. Make sure it is made of latex because there is some question as to whether other substances, such as vinyl, protect you from the HIV virus.

If you are engaging in oral sex of any kind, a latex barrier can be used also. A condom works fine on the penis. To place a barrier between a mouth and the vagina or anus, use something called a dental dam. This is a thin piece of latex used by dentists. If you have a hard time finding them, you can always cut a square of latex out of a latex glove and use that. It is a little thicker than a dental dam, but it will work fine. A little lubricant on the side opposite the mouth might make it more comfortable.

- If you are using a piece of S/M gear that might have come into contact with dangerous body fluids such as blood or ejaculate of another person, you should decontaminate that S/M toy before using it on another person. See the section below on decontamination of S/M gear.

- If an abrasion or cut results from a scene, it should be cleaned properly using a clean cloth or paper towel and an antibacterial agent, such as hydrogen peroxide. Covering the area with a clean bandage or gauze is often a good idea. If covering the area is not possible or advisable, just make sure to keep the area away from anything that might infect it (such as your hand).

Apart from potential person-to-person transmission of disease during S/M play, there is the additional risk of secondary transmission. In S/M, various gear is often used to enhance the play. If a piece of S/M gear is exposed to certain body fluids, such as blood or ejaculate, then used on another person, there is the potential risk that the diseases those body fluids can carry may be transferred to the next person the gear is used on. No one knows the degree of risk this involves. But the responsible S/M player must play on the side of caution.

One way to make sure to avoid such possible secondary transmission is to dedicate S/M toys to one person. If a piece of S/M equipment is only used on one person, there is no risk of infecting them with another person's body fluids via that piece of equipment. But if you do use S/M gear on more than one person, you should become familiar with the decontamination process.

The exact procedure you decide to use for decontaminating S/M gear may vary slightly as you refine it for yourself, but basically it requires these steps:

- Clean the object

- Rinse and dry the object

- Kill any possibly remaining virus or bacteria

- Clean the object again (if the viral/bacterial killing agent leaves a residue)

- Rinse and dry the object

- Condition the object

We'll use decontaminating a whip as an example. Let's say you whipped your partner and during the course of the scene the whip cut slightly into the skin, thereby possibly exposing the whip to your partner's blood. That whip must now be decontaminated before it is to be used on another person.

The first step is cleaning the object thoroughly. You will want to use a strong cleaning agent, perhaps one that has protein dissolving properties. Wash the object thoroughly, making sure to clean any part of the whip that might have come into contact with a person's body fluids. Next, rinse any excess cleaning agent off and dry the whip with a clean towel.

Now you must use a viral/bacterial killing agent. Hydrogen peroxide and 70% rubbing alcohol both work well, as does a 10% bleach solution which can be made with one part ordinary household bleach to nine parts water. All have been shown to kill the HIV virus on contact, so they're a good bet to use. Check with an AIDS eduction organization for other solutions they might recommend if you do not wish to use one of these. Remember that hydrogen peroxide turns to water shortly after exposure to light, so you might not want to use it on S/M gear that should not get wet much, like leather.

Likewise, the 10% bleach solution can ruin leather gear. 70% rubbing alcohol evaporates quickly and might be a better choice in some instances, such as on leather. Once again, soak all the parts of the whip that might have come into contact with body fluids. Let the whip stand for a few minutes.

Next, it is a good idea to rinse the object again and dry it thoroughly. Do not use the same portion of the clean towel you dried the whip with before. Sometimes paper towels work better for drying and applying any cleaning or viral/bacterial killing agents since they can be thrown away once used.

Since leather does not like such abuse, the whip (assuming it's made of leather) must be reconditioned to ensure the leather does not age and crack. Use a good leather dressing, perhaps one recommended by the person who sold you the leather.

Physical Safety

Apart from the health safety considerations, you must also insure the physical safety of all scene participants. Many of the physical safety concerns were addressed in the chapter on S/M technique, but here are some general guidelines that will serve you well in your S/M play.

- Slow down. Do not rush during S/M play. This can lead to mistakes and possible injury. Take your time.

- Police your play area. Is there anything that might injure you or your partner? How about sharp corners or objects someone might fall against? Is the floor slippery or littered with objects that might trip one of you? Is

138

the light adequate so you can see what you are doing?

- Never leave your partner alone. This is especially important if one of you is in bondage.

- Establish safe words and signals. Heed these words and signals at all times.

- Have a basic first aid kit handy and know how to use it.

- Trust your perceptions. If the scene appears not to be going quite right, stop. Now. Check in with your partner to make sure all is well. If it is not, correct the situation immediately.

- Have the local emergency phone number handy. If a serious injury occurs, do not hesitate to call that emergency number immediately. Believe me, emergency medical personnel have heard it all. There is nothing you could tell them that would shock them. The important thing is to get help fast if you need it.

- Do not play beyond your abilities. If you do not know how to do a certain type of scene, get as much information as you can first from another person experienced in that type of scene. Never let your pride push you into a scene you are not ready for. It's not worth it.

I strongly recommend you learn the basics of first aid and CPR. This is not only good advice for those interested in S/M, but for everyone. You never know when it might come in handy. Hopefully you will never need to use it, but being prepared is one of the cornerstones of safety.

The Red Cross or a similar organization in your area will likely have booklets on the subject of first aid and CPR. Call them up. Most such organizations will be glad to send information to you. If your local area has training programs available, sign up for them. Serious physical injury is not likely if S/M is done properly, but accidents do happen. It is your responsibility to be prepared. One of the books I recommend, The Lesbian S/M Safety Manual, has an excellent chapter on S/M first aid.

Emotional Safety

S/M is a highly charged emotional event for many people. As such, one must be aware of the need for emotional safety, not only for your partner, but for yourself as well. The taking or giving of erotic power to another human being is a big deal for most. Treat it with respect.

During a scene you may encounter a situation where a powerful emotional release happens. For example, if your partner was physically abused as a child, a hard spanking or whipping might release the emotional memories of those painful childhood events and cause the person to need lots of tenderness and support. In such situations, shut down the scene. Stop it immediately. Your only concern must be to ensure that the person experiencing those feelings feels loved and supported. Hold them. Talk if they wish to. Whatever you do, do not try to start the scene again too soon, if at all. The best course of action might be to stop playing altogether and spend some quality quiet time with that person.

If you are the person who needs the emotional support,

ask for it from your partner. If they won't give it to you, they're not worth playing with. Stop the scene yourself, leave and call a trusted friend or psychotherapeutic professional. Above all, take care of yourself. You deserve it.

Most situations in which emotions might need attention during a scene are not nearly as urgent as the example above. That does not mean, however, that they don't need attending to. They do. If you have an emotional issue you need to discuss with your partner, do so. Negative emotions will undoubtedly get in the way of enjoyment of the scene anyway. You might as well clear the air immediately.

If a scene elicits a particularly positive emotional response, it can be important to talk about that also. The bottom line is that S/M partners must take care of each other's emotional needs before, during and after play. That kind of responsibility comes with the territory.

Remember that unless you are a psychotherapeutic professional, you are not qualified to handle serious emotional trauma, whether it is your own or that of your partner. If you or your partner appears to have serious emotional issues to deal with, consultation with a professional is a good idea. However, if your emotional issues deal in any way with S/M itself, or if you feel you must talk about your S/M to a professional to process your issues, you need to find one who understands S/M.

The acceptance of safe, sane and consensual S/M is happening at an increasing rate among psychotherapeutic professionals, but many still believe it to be a pathological problem. I believe that will change in the future, just as therapeutic views on homosexuality have changed in the recent past. But if you have problems now, you need help now. Finding an S/M-friendly professional is not always easy, but it can be done.

The best way to find such a professional is to get a referral from someone within the S/M community. Ask everyone in the S/M community you know for references. Once you get the name of a referral, make an appointment to talk with that professional. Make appointments with others if you get more than one referral. When you have that first appointment, remember that you are interviewing them. You have to decide if they can help you and part of that decision may be based on their attitudes about S/M. Don't be bullied. You are paying them for their services and you deserve to procure a therapist who can understand you and your life choices.

Chapter 12

THE NEXT STEP

You've learned a great deal by reading this book. But just reading about S/M without actually playing is a little like reading a cookbook without ever cooking. It might provide a modicum of titillating distraction, but ultimately it won't be very satisfying if that's all you do.

It's time to play!

If you currently have a partner who wishes to explore S/M with you, wonderful. The time to begin that exploration is now. If they haven't read this book, you might suggest that they do. That way you'll both be starting out with the same foundation. If they don't wish to read the book, tell them some of the highlights and answer their questions. Your partner may believe a lot of the misconceptions about S/M that so many other people believe. Allay their fears. Tell them the truth about S/M and how it can be a loving and sensual act of lovemaking between two people who care about each other.

If you do not currently have a partner to explore S/M with, go find one. Don't rush it, though. You want to make sure they're the right person for you. Use the tips and guidelines in this book and search out a potential playmate. Once you've found them, nurture the relationship.

Try to learn more about S/M. Seek out resources of learning such as S/M support organizations or good S/M reading material. And always remember that no matter how much you learn about S/M, there's always more to learn.

Chapter 13

CONCLUSION

S/M is lovemaking. Hopefully, that is the message you have gotten from this book. Now is the time for S/M to take its rightful place among the accepted variations partners may choose from to express their affections. Now is the time for each person to claim their right to individual erotic expression. Now is the time for you to have the satisfying realization of your fantasies that you deserve.

Be safe, be sane, be consensual. And most of all, have fun!

THE S/M RESOURCES GUIDE

When I first began writing this book, I imagined that it would contain a complete resource guide to S/M in the appendix. It would list retail outlets, magazines, books, S/M events, bars, and organizations, to name just a few. As I began compiling the resource list, I soon realized that immediately after the book was published, the listing would be obsolete, or at best incomplete. Things change too fast for such a listing to remain current for long.

So I decided to make the S/M resources listing available separately. It is published under the name of The S/M Resources Guide and is available by mail through the publisher of this book. The S/M Resources Guide is updated and revised regularly, thereby providing current information to those using it. It is published in very simple photocopied form, allowing extreme flexibility in keeping the listings up to date.

You can obtain a copy of The S/M Resources Guide by sending your name and address, along with a check or money order in the amount of $9.95 (payable to "Daedalus Publishing Company") to:

Daedalus Publishing Company
Attn: Resources Guide
4470-107 Sunset Boulevard, Suite 375
Los Angeles, CA 90027 USA

California residents should add 8.25% sales tax and $2.50 shipping and handling. For your convenience, an order form is provided at the back of this book.

Anyone wishing to have a listing included in The S/M

Resources Guide is also welcome to submit that listing, in writing, to the above address.

RECOMMENDED READING

The author recommends the following books for those wishing to learn more about S/M.

Leatherfolk, edited by Mark Thompson, Alyson Publications, 40 Plympton Street, Boston, MA. A series of excellent essays written by experts in the leather/SM/ fetish community.

Masochism - A Jungian View, by Lyn Cowan, Spring Publications, Inc., P.O. Box 222069, Dallas, Texas 75222. A beautifully written work by a Jungian analyst presenting a new theory of masochism.

The Lesbian S/M Safety Manual, edited by Pat Califia, Lace Publications, 40 Plympton Street, Boston, Massachusetts 02118. An excellent compilation written by women on various S/M topics.

S/M - The Last Taboo, by Gerald and Caroline Greene, Grove Press, Inc., 53 East 11th Street, New York, New York 10003. One of the first modern books on S/M. A bit academic in style, but a good study of S/M at the time it was written. The appendix contains some entertaining S/M literary pieces.

Studies in Sadomasochism, edited by Thomas Weinberg and G.W. Levi Kamel, Prometheus Books, 700 East Amherst Street, Buffalo, New York 14214. A collection of scholarly essays about S/M.

Urban Aboriginals, by Geoff Mains, Gay Sunshine Press, P.O. Box 40397, San Francisco, California 94140. An intelligent and sensitive exploration of the gay men's leather/SM subculture.

Coming to Power - Writings and Graphics on Lesbian S/M, edited by Samois, Alyson Publications, 40 Plympton St., Boston, MA 02118. A collection of writings, information, and graphics about S/M.

GLOSSARY

The S/M scene has a language all its own. This section will hopefully help the newcomer understand jargon associated with the S/M scene.

Abbreviations — Often S/M personal ads contain abbreviations for descriptions or activities the person likes. Some of these are listed below.

B/D or BD — Bondage and discipline
S/M or SM — Sadomasochism
TT — Tit Torture (nipple play)
FF — Fist Fucking
TV — Transvestite or Transvestism
TS — Transsexual
L/L or LL — Leather/Levi
CBT or C&BT — Cock and ball torture
VA — Verbal Abuse
WS — Water Sport (piss)

Abrasion — The use of skin surface sensations produced by a rubbing motion for erotic effect.

Ass Play — Erotic playing with the anal area.

Bondage — The restraining of the body in some way for erotic stimulation.

Bottom — Someone who enjoys the submissive role in an S/M scene. However, those who play with more subtle power exchanges may consider Bottom to mean the passive partner in a scene.

Breath Control — This is erotic enjoyment derived from the controlling of access to air during breathing. The dangers here are evident — you or your partner could suffocate. This is a very dangerous type of play and should not be engaged in by anyone who has not been in the scene for many years. Most S/M players stay away from this type of play altogether.

Captivity — The enjoyment of simulated captivity. For example, someone might assume the role of prisoner during an S/M scene.

Catheterization — Technique of inserting medical catheters into the urethra for erotic effect.

Cutting — The cutting of the skin for erotic enjoyment. The cuts are usually very superficial. It is done only by one highly skilled in this technique, using sterile equipment.

Cross Dressing — Enjoyment from dressing in the style of the opposite sex — man as woman or woman as man.

Dental Dam — A small, thin latex sheet used in dental procedures. Makes a great safe sex barrier during certain kinds of oral sex.

Dildo — An erotic device, usually made of rubber, specifically intended for insertion into either the vaginal or anal cavity.

Dominant — One who is dominant. This term is more often used in the heterosexual S/M community than the gay and lesbian S/M community.

Domination — The exertion of control over another person for the erotic enjoyment of both.

Electricity — A form of S/M play involving the use of static or AC/DC electricity to stimulate the body. (See Relaxacisor and Ultra Violet Wand.)

Exhibitionism — Erotic pleasure from displaying oneself erotically in front of one or more people.

Fisting — Insertion of the hand into the anal or vaginal cavity.

Flagellation — Describes a wide variety of S/M activities involving the striking of the body with an implement or the hand. For example, whipping, paddling, caning, and spanking.

Genitorture — Torturing (erotic torture, of course) of the genitals during S/M play.

Hot Wax — The dripping of hot wax from a candle onto the body for erotic play. Beeswax candles should never be used because they melt at a higher temperature and might leave blisters.

Humiliation — A type of S/M scene where humiliation of the partner is the goal. Care must be taken to make sure that this aspect of the scene is fantasy-based and not taken by the humiliated partner as sincere lowering of self-esteem.

Infantilism — Erotic pleasure from things having to do with infancy and young childhood. Role playing, with one or both adults assuming the roles of an infant or young child, is common. This is not to be confused with pedophilia, which is the erotic enjoyment of children, which is not condoned in any way by this book or by any responsible member of the S/M community.

Leatherman — A term originated in the gay men's community for men interested in leather and/or S/M. A leatherman may, or may not, be interested in S/M. A leatherman's style of dress is typically a stylized version of stereotypical biker garb.

Leatherwoman — A term originated in the lesbian community for women interested in leather and/or S/M. A leatherwoman may, or may not, be interested in S/M. A leatherwoman's style of dress is typically a stylized version of stereotypical biker garb.

Masochist — One who enjoys the receiving of intense physical S/M stimulation.

153

Master — A man who assumes the role of one with total control over the submissive partner (slave) in an S/M scene.

Mistress — A woman who assumes the role of one with total control over the submissive partner (slave) in an S/M scene.

Mummification — A special kind of bondage experience where the body is wrapped in a fashion similar to an Egyptian mummy. Often parts of the body are left exposed for erotic play.

Negotiation — The negotiating of ground rules between partners who are going to engage in S/M play. Vital to the maintenance of safe, sane and consensual play.

Piercing — The inserting of needles into the body for erotic effect. The piercing can be temporary or permanent. Permanent piercings are maintained by inserting various kinds of piercing jewlery.

Play Party — A party of people interested in S/M at which attendees engage in S/M play with others at the party. Not at all like an orgy, since most partners couple up and play exclusively together. Many play parties are equipped with an array of large pieces of S/M equipment for the use of attendees.

Relaxacisor — An electric device used to stimulate muscles as a form of passive exercise. It can be used for S/M play, but should never be used above the waist. This could cause interference with the normal electrical action of the heart.

Role Playing — Assuming roles (master/slave, doctor/patient, police officer/prisoner, etc.) during an S/M scene.

S/M (S&M) — A safe, sane, consensual, and fun erotic encounter where the exchange of power between the partners is a principal element.

Sadist — One who enjoys the giving of intense physical S/M stimulation to another.

Safe Word — A word, or group of words, used to indicate something to the other partner in an S/M scene. For example, the word green might mean go, yellow slow, and red stop. When one partner hears the other say a safe word, they are obligated to abide by what that word signals.

Safe, Sane and Consensual — The credo by which much of the S/M community plays. It must be safe, sane and consensual or it is not S/M.

Safe Signal — A signal, or group of signals, used to indicate something to the other partner in an S/M scene. For example, snapping the fingers might mean to stop the action and pause to talk about it. When one partner hears the other give a safe signal, they are obligated to abide by what that signal means.

Scene — (1) An S/M play session. (2) A reference to the S/M community as a whole. For example, you might ask someone if they are part of the "scene".

Sensory Deprivation — Depriving one or more of a person's senses (sight, hearing, touch, taste, smell) to produce a heightened erotic state.

Shaving — The shaving of the body as erotic stimulation.

Slave — One who enjoys submission, with that submission being deep enough to elicit the feeling of being owned or fully controlled by the dominant partner.

Submission — The release of control over oneself, to whatever extent, for the erotic pleasure of both the submissive and dominant partners.

Submissive — One who is submissive during an S/M encounter. This term is more often used in the heterosexual S/M community than the gay and lesbian S/M community.

Switch — A term used to describe someone who enjoys both dominant and submissive roles.

Tit Clamps — An S/M toy that places pressure on the nipples for erotic stimulation.

Top — Someone who enjoys the dominant role in an S/M scene. However, those who play with more subtle power exchanges may consider Top to mean the active partner in a scene.

Torture — What this refers to is erotic torture. What a person actually experiences may really be anything but torture to them, but the word often fuels their fantasy. Often the appearance of non-consensuality is an important factor (but, of course, it is actually consensual).

Ultra Violet Wand — This is an electric device consisting of a handle attached to a glass tube, filled with a gas, and charged with an electric current. The tube glows with a violet color when turned on. When placed near the skin, it sends out a mild spark. It was originally created to help stimulate the scalp. Its abilities to stimulate the scalp may be questionable, but it makes a great S/M toy. It should never be used above the neck.

Urethral Sound — A surgical stainless steel device used in the medical field. Used in S/M scenes for insertion into the urethra.

Verbal Abuse — The use of strong abusive language as a fantasy element in an S/M scene.

Water Sports — The erotic enjoyment of urine or urination.

ABOUT THE AUTHOR

Race Bannon is a nationally recognized expert in S/M, devoting much of his time to furthering the understanding of safe, sane and consensual S/M sexuality. He has written articles, facilitated seminars and workshops, and lectured throughout the United States about S/M.

If you wish to contact him for speaking engagements or interviews, you may reach him in writing in care of the publisher.

Available from Daedalus Publishing Company

BOOKS

Ties That Bind
The SM/Leather/Fetish Erotic Style
Issues, Commentaries and Advice

The writings of one of the most respected and knowledgeable people on the subject of the SM/leather/fetish erotic style has been compiled in this book. Issues regarding relationships, the community, the SM experience, and personal transformation, as they relate to this form of erotic play, are addressed. The author, Guy Baldwin, is a well-known psychotherapist whose clients include many men and women who engage in this form of erotic play. Unlike many in the mental health field, Mr. Baldwin takes the approach that this style of erotic play can definitely be part of a healthy expression of one's sexuality. Many have benefited from his sound advice in seminars, workshops, and through his many published articles. Now, much of this man's wisdom has been published for you in this book. Price: $14.95

Learning the Ropes
A Basic Guide to Safe and Fun S/M Lovemaking

Curious about S/M? Perhaps you have always had an interest but did not know where to find reliable information. Or perhaps you just want to enhance your lovemaking with a spouse or partner. Whatever your reason for an interest in S/M, this book can help. This concise book guides the reader through the basics of safe and fun S/M. Learn what S/M is, how to do it safely, and how to connect with partners, plus much more. Written by S/M expert Race Bannon. Destined to become a classic in its field. Price: $12.95

The Master's Manual
A Handbook of Erotic Dominance

The idea of erotically dominating a partner appeals to many men and women. Unfortunately, there have been few resources from which to learn how to do this in a safe, fun, and responsible way. Now there is *The Master's Manual*. Author Jack Rinella examines various aspects of erotic dominance including SM, safety, sex, erotic power, techniques, and much more. Even if your primary interest is erotic submission rather than dominance, this book will give you insights that will help lead you to a more fulfilling sexuality. The author speaks in a clear, frank, and nonjudgmental way to any man or woman, regardless of sexual orientation, with an interest in the erotic dominant/submissive dynamic. Price: $14.95

The Leather Contest Guide
A Handbook for Promoters, Contestants, Judges and Titleholders

This is truly the complete guide to the leather contest. Contest promoters, contestants, judges and winners will all benefit from the sound advice presented in this book. Written by Guy Baldwin, one of the most famous names in the leather community and a former titleholder, this book clearly details the keys to a successful leather contest. Even those in the audience will enjoy the insights this book will give about the world of the leather contest. Price: $12.95

OTHER PUBLICATIONS

The S/M Resources Guide

Where do you find S/M equipment stores, mail order suppliers, leather craftspeople, S/M-oriented books and magazines, computer bulletin boards catering to the S/M community, S/M clubs and organizations, lists of S/M community events, or anything else related to your S/M interests? Now you can turn to The S/M Resources Guide. This guide is updated regularly, sometimes daily, and supplied to you in photocopied form so that you will have the most current information possible. Price: $9.95

How to Make Rope Restraints

Leather wrist and ankle restraints are common toys used during S/M play. But these types of restraints are expensive and don't always fit comfortably. Race Bannon has developed these instructions for making a set of rope restraints that function much like the more expensive leather restraints, but with more versatility and comfort. Rope restraints are comfortable, inexpensive, and will adjust to any size wrist or ankle. With these instructions, and a few dollars worth of rope, you can construct a set of four restraints in just minutes. Price: $3.95

ORDERING INFORMATION

To order any of the above publications, send your name, mailing address, and the names of the publications you wish, along with a check or money order made payable to "Daedalus Publishing Company." Do not send cash. Our mailing address is Daedalus Publishing Company, 4470-107 Sunset Boulevard, Suite 375, Los Angeles, CA 90027 USA.

California residents should add 8.25% sales tax. All orders should include a shipping and handling charge of $2.50 added to the total of the entire order.